A Sea Less Traveled

In Pursuit of Orcinus Orca

Millennial Mind Publishing
An imprint of American Book Publishing
American Book Publishing
P.O. Box 65624
Salt Lake City, UT 84165
www.american-book.com
Printed in the United States of America on acid-free paper.

A Sea Less Traveled
In Pursuit of Orcinus Orcas

Designed by Jana Rade, design@american-book.com

Publisher's Note: *This publication is designed to provide accurate and authoritative information in regard to the subject matter covered. It is sold or distributed with the understanding that the publisher and author is not engaged in rendering legal, accounting, or other professional service. If legal advice or other expert assistance is required, the services of a competent professional person in a consultation capacity should be sought.*

ISBN 1-58982-208-0

Pillsbury, Patrick, A Sea Less Traveled: In Pursuit of Orcinus Orcas

---

Special Sales

These books are available at special discounts for bulk purchases. Special editions, including personalized covers, excerpts of existing books, and corporate imprints, can be created in large quantities for special needs. For more information e-mail orders@american-book.com, 801-486-8639.

A Sea Less Traveled

In Pursuit of Orcinus Orca

Patrick Pillsbury

Dedication

To my three daughters.

Preface

A Sea Less Traveled—why did you write the book? Good question and one I am not sure I know the answer to. It started with an appreciation for a thirty-foot wooden boat that grew the more time I spent on her. From the first day I laid eyes on her, she tugged at my heartstrings.

Over time, our relationship took on a human side. No, I didn't hear voices from her holds or see ghostly images in her berths; it was subtle changes in my own attitude that were brought about by the *Bon Accord*. It was as if she captured me in admiration. In turn, feeling not worthy of her, she brought me to question my life and my pursuits in life. Her qualities I so admired were the same qualities I lacked in chasing my goals.

I learned from the *Bon Accord* patience, perseverance, the love of exploration, and other qualities that I once knew, had somewhat abandoned, and longed to rediscover.

Fueled in a large part by the beauty of the San Juan Islands, a spiritual place of sorts, I sought to question my past, look for something to grab hold of, and analyze what the future may bring. In touring the islands, and being engulfed in the simple balance that exists within the waters, I questioned my sense of value and worth as it relates to life's chase. My favorite line in the book is one I hope rings a theme throughout: "A seal looks for no bigger a rock from which to rest and an eagle no bigger a branch from which to peer."

So along the way I looked to answer a nagging question: what in us drives us to bigger rocks and better branches? Being by nature more to the rule than the exception on this, I looked to find the answer to this riddle. After all, the *Bon Accord* is both bigger and better than a lot of other boats.

Along the way I came across the orcas, Orcinus orca. Tour after tour I watched passengers, and learned their motivations, their reasons for coming to see one of the largest ocean predators in the world. In turn, I found parallels to my questions in life and that of the fate of the orcas.

To me, part of the answer lies in our youth—those uninhibited years we felt a special sensation in our minds, a "giddy" feeling that made us feel unique and special in our own eyes. It may have been a fleeting moment or perhaps longer, but the spectacular nature of it all was the same. I feel we're all in search of the "giddy" feeling—moments where boundaries cease and overwhelming feelings of joy persist. Only in our youth were these feelings unabated, with no ramifications or restraints or higher education to check these emotions.

The orcas provide this same sensation for many, a chance to reconnect to the "giddy" feeling. Awed by their power and grace, we, for a fleeting moment, become caught up in our emotions, lost to thought, lost to worry. But is our thirst for this emotion too grand? In our pursuits to be up close and within reach of the orcas, do we forsake their welfare?

A Sea Less Traveled…is about the relationship between the *Bon Accord*, her captain, and the orcas. The common thread of human emotion as captured onboard the *Bon Accord* spins an interesting fate for each, their future inexorably tied together in pursuit of Orcinus orca.

Introduction

The San Juan Islands are a tightly knit group of islands about seventy miles north of Seattle, along the British Columbia border. In the early 1960s there was believed to be around 100-plus orcas in the southern resident pods of the San Juan Islands. Today, they number eighty-three total whales, slightly more than a few years back when they suffered a 20 percent loss in population over a five-year period. The reason for their decline, namely toxins (PCBs, mercury...) and a lack of food source due to increased population around Puget Sound and weather phenomena such as El Niño, which has a dramatic effect on the salmon runs in the area.

The socioeconomic impact of whale watching in the San Juan Islands in a large part fuels the economic activity on the islands. People come from all over the world to catch a glimpse of the most heralded of marine mammals, Orcinus orca, killer whale. They board ferries on the U.S. mainland, fly in seaplanes, charter private boats—hundreds of thousands come each year, spending millions of dollars.

A fleet of boats serves the trade, taking passengers out daily from towns in and around the San Juans. Commercial whale watching boats, fishing boats, pleasure craft, and research vessels leave Friday Harbor, Anacortes, and other small towns within an hour or two of San Juan Island.

The *Bon Accord* is thirty-foot wooden trawler, built in the San Juan Islands. She has plied her trade, charter boat, for fifteen years here in the waters the orcas swim. Her captain, at age thirty-eight, has moved to the islands in search of a more simple life, one free from the pressures and consumption inherent in an urban setting.

Through the *Bon Accord*, the islands are perceived in a magical existence for those onboard, one that brings about an appreciation for the islands and its inhabitants, orcas included. In turn, it warrants attention to the fate of the orcas, empowers her captain to learn of their past, and seeks knowledge that will bring those who board the *Bon Accord* to look for lessons in life, not just amusement.

The islands are magical, with their pristine bays, lone beaches, and stretches of evergreens standing tall along her shores. The *Bon Accord*, while traveling her paths, records each and every thought that transpires from those onboard, learning of her fate, the fate of the islands, the fate of the orcas, and all else that passes her bow.

Table of Contents

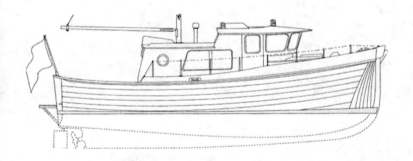

Bon Accord

Bon Accord

I purchased the *Bon Accord* the summer of 2002, not purely as a means to escape suburbia and city life, although this was highly sought. And it certainly wasn't for a windfall of income. I sit here typing, wondering if the silent phone is due to a lack of charter business or whether I paid the phone bill this month.

There was something else about the *Bon Accord* that allured me into making an offer on a sixteen-year-old wooden charter boat, nestled among the ever growing fleet of "plastic fantastics"—molded fiberglass boats that more closely resemble a used bar of soap than an oceangoing vessel. I knew as I approached her she spoke sincere, humbly in her slip, a big puppy dog. I couldn't resist; I had to embark on her journey. Exactly what that journey was, or where it would lead me, was a mystery. Nonetheless, it was a passage I had to make.

She had it all, the *Bon Accord*; her lines were smooth, her look unique—much like my wife of eight years. Although I can't say the boat arouses the same sensation amidships as my wife, she does come close.

I'd always been one to stop and glance at a felled-timber-turned-boat. Whether tied to mooring, decaying in a boatyard, neglected at anchor, or plying through the water, I always felt that wooden boats spoke volumes about their owners, their trade, and life in general. Wooden boats have a human side to them. Crafted by artists and sailed by seamen, each with an appreciation for the living medium from which their passions are derived.

At thirty feet in length, ten feet in width, and four feet in depth, the *Bon Accord* is a classic northwest trawler, sturdy from stem to stern. A low profile cabin, sweeping sheer, and humble accommodations give her the characteristics and blue-collar appearance of a workboat. Like the men who first explored the Northwest and those that followed to claim her bounty, she has the look of determination, a steely resolve to meet life head-on and leave as little a wake as possible in return.

The *Bon Accord* was penciled by the famed Canadian naval architect, William Garden, and crafted by onetime local Orcas Island boat-builder, Krist Martinsen, in 1986. I'd always admired Bill Garden's boats, his approach to balancing historical yacht design and art. Taking working boat lines and giving them more appeal through sweeping sheer lines, plumb bows, and graceful houses. I'm privy to this daily on the *Bon Accord*, always taking a step back to bring in her lines as I leave the dock, perhaps seeking her out, looking for her to impart some guidance or wisdom.

She is of cold-molded construction, three-fourth inch fir planks laminated together, a chine hull with sawn frames on stations, and longitudinal to take the double skin planking. Frames and planks are cured with a thick epoxy resin and laid at forty-five-degree angles to each other. She is fitted out with bronze fittings and deck hardware. One particular feature, that often escapes the minds of designers today, is a wraparound deck that circles the cabin house, allowing one the ability to circumnavigate the boat without ever going inside. Today, boats are built for purchase on a showroom floor, "zero percent financing and no money down." Large accommodations filled with fine Corinthian leather spill over their girth, leaving one to grab a rail and tight walk it up to the bow if and when the boats ever leave the dock.

In contrast, every inch of the *Bon Accord* is spoken for. Upon entering her cabin house, one finds a water closet or marine head (toilet) just to port, forward of which lies a settee or L-shaped eating area suited for four adults. To starboard sits a galley with refrigerator, gimballed stove, and sink. Toward the bow, just forward of amidships, a raised pilothouse with forward slant windows provides excellent visibility across 180 degrees, followed by a sunken or lowered forward bunk or V-berth room. Like all well-designed boats, everything seems to have a place onboard, with no wasted square footage nor unnecessary appliances or equipment. And just enough drawers, closet space, and cupboards to stow only what is needed.

The best compliment I've heard paid to her, was the idea that when one viewed her in a photo, they had trouble estimating what size boat she was. Her lines, features, and overall appearance is all to scale. She may look thirty feet or even up to fifty feet in a photo, no easy task to assign to a thirty-foot boat that sleeps four. There are no oversized windows, enlarged doorways, or undersized cleats and deck hardware, which are common on most manufactured boats these days. Nor does she have any right angles; her decks, her cabin, and her topsides all gently slope or angle so no one spot stands out. She is worthy of admiration from all angles, not just when viewed thirty degrees off her bow.

Her interior is trimmed out with teak and mahogany, around greenish-gray painted surfaces of marine plywood. Brass light fixtures and a few bronze fittings are evenly spaced throughout. A Boston clock and barometer sit over the settee. In the pilothouse, she is equipped with JRC radar, Garmin GPS, Raytheon VHF radio and a handful of other electronics including a Sitex depth sounder and a Ritchie compass. We've made only slight changes, ripping up Formica counters and replacing them with fourth-inch by two-inch teak strips, and replacing badly worn fabric in the settee with a wide whale blue cord. Other projects are still in the works. She has a warm feel below, a curl-up-and-read warmth to her— a boat that when onboard, you don't feel as though you need to leave the dock. Your focus is inward, reflecting on the beauty within her lines. She is a work of art.

She is powered by a John Deere 108 horsepower, turbo, marine diesel engine with nearly 8,000 hours on her. Her engine rests in the aft cockpit floor near the stern, with an insulated engine box which doubles as cockpit seating over top. A Walters V-drive redirects the shaft back toward the stern, reducing the vibration and noise in the cabin. Without the V-drive, the engine would need to be positioned just under the settee, making for a louder and somewhat shakier cabin.

Her controls, steering, and all other mechanical facets are perfectly located, easy to work on, and offer little trouble. From her perched pilothouse, I often sit in admiration of just how well she is laid out, how the use of trim and the proportions were each carefully crafted with precision. Is there more to this? A human dimension I seek to learn?

Over the past year, I've learned from her patient, caring, and humble approach to the seas. Sometimes, questioning my approach to life in comparison. She meets waves head-on, brushing them off with a purpose, using her plumb bow and high sweep of sheer forward, as if to say, "bring it on." Her low freeboard aft and modest stern section in departing with a humble appreciation for the challenge is unlike many of her plastic counterparts that leave turmoil in their large wakes— spewing exhaust, and turning a grotesque stern section as they race in delight for their owners' next Bloody Mary.

I wish for her control, her resolve. Rarely she needs only the slightest turn of her helm to set her course. What in us alters our course, spins our wheel, sets us in motion toward a goal? At the wheel of the *Bon Accord*, can I too sail a steady course through life's tides?

Being of wood construction, she has a warm feel and ride through the water like no other material, absorbing waves and sound, rather than pounding over them. Those who have heard the crack of a wooden bat at the ballpark and the ping of their aluminum counterpart across Little League fields everywhere can relate. Of course, the connection to nature, and to the art inherent in the building of a wooden boat, all add value in the eyes of their owners, myself included. But was there more to the *Bon Accord*? Had I carried an aluminum bat through life to date, failing to absorb life, to hear the sounds of nature, the crack of life? Had my ears been deafened by the "chink" of metal?

The *Bon Accord* is one of a few wooden boats in the whale watching fleet off the San Juan Islands. Most have gone the route of low maintenance behemoths—designed for the sole purpose of maximizing profits—on the one end, to small inflatable boats with maximum horsepower and bugs in the teeth on the other. I had worked for large global conglomerates, behemoths in their world, and I had worked for fast paced independents. Had I missed out, failed to find my "wooden boat" in life, one that offered harmony in the working world?

She has her weaknesses or what some may perceive as such. She is the slowest boat in the fleet, a characteristic that doesn't escape the eye or occasional ribbing of other captains. At eight knots cruising speed, she churns along, content within herself. To push her at ten knots, she tries, but her motion is interrupted, her flow distracted. She raises her bow to the challenge, but her frames resist. It's a novel idea—go slow, and seek life out. Has she empowered me with patience so soon?

Underway, there is nothing more soothing than the sound of water lapping up against her wood hull. I've heard it said that water, when interrupted or altered in flow, creates negative ions, which in turn create a positive aura around you. Is this what draws us to the orcas? We're all in search of the everlasting negative ion? I've felt the same sensation many times. Pouring a Guinness into a frothy pint glass, taking a hot shower after a cold day on the water, or casting a fly into a rumbling creek on a hot day.

Bon Accord

I know the *Bon Accord* feels the aura as her plumb bow slices through the swells. Her somewhat flared entry, redirecting water out and away from the boat for the pleasure of those she carries onboard, rather than up or back. It's a pretty sound, not a hard smack nor jolt, like millions of tiny particles of glass cascading off her in unison, in tune with her motion as she meets oncoming seas.

Waves are steep in Puget Sound—not big, the troughs or distance between the waves short in comparison to their ocean-crossing cousins. Shallow water and currents refuse any uniformity or consistency in flow around the islands. Is this why the *Bon Accord* so reflects her surroundings? Small by comparison to her oceangoing sisters, yet she is tough and sturdy.

She greets oncoming seas with a passion, each with the same enthusiasm as the last…short bursts of fury as she rises and glances waves off, followed by even shorter moments of uncertainty as her bow free-falls into the abyss that seems to exists between challenges. I wonder how she feels this moment, this abyss? Does she revel in thought like a prizefighter between rounds, twitch in jubilation like a grade-schooler who has just spelled "a-n-e-m-o-n-e" in the school bee?

At the wheel, it's not the size of the wave that creates that knot in your stomach, but the uncertainty of what follows, the moment the wave passes under her hull at your feet. Perhaps we find comfort in things we may measure? A wave stands before us, exists before our eyes. An abyss is an unknown, secret destiny—insecurity prevails. It's a brief moment; the *Bon Accord*'s bow falls—it's not the distance, but the silence of just how far she will plummet. And when you hit the trough, her bow disappears into a sea of green water before your eyes, horizon lost, moments flash. She rises from these depths proud, water everywhere, inhaling, soaring up to the next challenge. Is this what the orcas feel with each breath? Do they feel the abyss between waves? The uncertainty of what lies over the next wave?

I can offer the *Bon Accord* relief in the bigger seas on days when it blows by turning the wheel slightly to port or to starboard, offering her to the waves at a slight angle in order to lengthen the trough or time between swells. However, in these conditions every so often she'll playfully jump off a wave, one I've yet to gauge or measure, catching me by surprise before I've had a chance to turn her away. It's these waves that loosen up that knot in your stomach, and create that queasy feeling in your midsection. I fear for the boat's condition at times—a loosening of her seams, a weakening of her frames. I also fear the day my passengers sense the brief anxiety in my gaze as I trail off in thought to sounds of timber cracking and machines breaking; I'm fearful they'll sense a weakness in their captain, and experience a sudden longing to be somewhere else that day.

In following seas, those that approach from astern, it's a different sensation vs. taking waves on the bow, though no less thought provoking. Unfortunately, being of deep-V construction she needs quite the push from the seas to launch her into a planing or surfing motion down the waves, an occurrence rarely encumbered in the San Juans. The archipelago is sheltered from the ocean swells that parade down the coast from the Gulf of Alaska. However, the prevailing winds do come from the southwest, up the sound from Seattle, and we do see rollers off the west side of San Juan Island in Haro Strait on occasion.

It's a fine line between the elation that comes from surfing down a wave and the white knuckles of the paying passengers onboard, in turn a liability.

It's a sweet feel, though, and a playful one when the *Bon Accord* lifts her stern to greet a five- to seven-foot swell with crested whitecaps, dips her bow, and readies herself in appreciation for the challenge. It is a moment when all is still. All is quiet onboard. It's a brief but great moment. Sailors, surfers, and seamen alike know the feeling. It's as if the *Bon Accord* is floating on a cloud; water has evaporated through her planks. It's that moment where in our youth we gasped as the roller coaster reached its peak, before plummeting to the ground.

The ensuing rush is anything but still as she takes off on her own accord, free from restraints imposed upon her by design—those same restraints that make her so comfortable meeting seas (deep-V) head-on. Initially, it's hard to notice the transition, but soon the sensation of cascading or surfing down a wave is felt in her frames. She is light at the wheel, gliding, jubilant in motion, bow out of the water, charging into the trough that separates her and her next challenge.

I've looked for comparisons in life to these moments, bits and pieces of time where cares cease to exist; an unfettered willingness to charge on drowns out any feelings of insecurity within. The *Bon Accord* charges down wave after wave, not worried about the abyss within each trough or the strain on her planks; she's at peace in her world.

I've felt the sensation at times: in youth as fears were conquered, in the teens through a first kiss, and as of late more and more I seem to enjoy them through my children. Is it the hint of fear that creates this sensation? In youth we fear obstacles, mountains, heights, falling—objects that offer physical hurt if we fail to conquer or stumble. In adolescence we fear emotional pain, hurt from within. In adulthood, we fear most for our children's safety. Do we long for that fear we felt in our youths? Do we seek the presence of orcas for their power, their ability to make us feel that fear we felt in our youth—vulnerable—so we become lost for a brief moment in their presence, charging down our own waves free of guilt? How do we transition from this brief moment back to reality?

The *Bon Accord* slows back into the trough, dips her stern—exhale—awaits the next swell—inhale—to lift her into utopia again. Do we sail through life in troughs?

Unfortunately, surfing down waves on the *Bon Accord* is few and far between. In most cases, short-lived as well, only to be followed by one of the more cruel conditions: seas from abeam, seas that meet the *Bon Accord* from ninety degrees off her bow.

The *Bon Accord* is eleven feet in width; a wave of three to five feet need only seconds to pass under. Yet, the *Bon Accord* exposes her flanks in these short gaps, heaving her flat broadsides toward each ensuing spanking. She jerks, slaps, pushes on out of rhythm; it's painful to expose her to these conditions, and in turn, exposing the passengers onboard. I suppose these are her bad days, the moments when she is not in harmony with the sea, she complains little, offers no regret, seeks no sympathy. What in us makes us seek to impose our burdens on others, instead of steaming on, bow up?

Bon Accord

To help her along in these seas, I've added a steadying sail to her rig, eighteen square feet of tanbark canvas, located just aft her cabin. The luff or leading edge of the sail is run up her mast, a ten-foot spar of spruce anchored to her cabin top, which up until now was used for signal flags and navigational lights. A boom made of the same serves to anchor the clew or trailing edge of the sail and two jury-rigged sheets or lines are used to trim her to the wind.

The sail, by design, is intended to ease her motion, to counter the relatively low center of gravity of the *Bon Accord*. In theory the sail acts as a counterweight, creating resistance in the direction the *Bon Accord* is rolling, ideally slowing the motion to a gentle roll versus a not-so-gentle jarring motion. In practice, a sail of less than twenty square feet offers little to a boat weighing in at over 11,500 pounds, so my sail of sorts may prove to aid more in appearance than practice. Nonetheless, I've always been a sailor at heart, so she affords me some security within, a link to my past.

Is it possible to learn life's lessons through a onetime living medium? Have I purchased the *Bon Accord* as a means to support my family, deliver them from suburbia to an Eden of sorts? Or have I, in choosing to follow her path, opened my soul to her, looked for her advice, and sought within her what I had failed to learn of myself to date?

So, we sail on, I at the wheel, she beneath and all around me. What of our fate, a sea less traveled, a dream realized, a fear conquered?

Her Captain

It's on odd existence when we travel paths only dreamed of in years past. Taking a flyer, choosing a sea less traveled. What inside us drives us to make these choices?

We strive to meet our basic needs, those cornered in the triangle of life: food and shelter, safety and health. But what of our pursuits, to what do we owe our Maker? In an ever-increasing world of marketing and consumption, can one simplify? It looks good painted on a sign in a catalogue.

Prior to purchasing the *Bon Accord*, I spent the better part of my adult life in search of a career. Twelve years in a suit bouncing from one sales position to another, the grass was always greener elsewhere, I was certain. I sat in sales meetings, flew around the country, met with top executives. All the while never really believing it was the path I was destined to take or follow. I awoke each day, drove to work, spent hours on the phone, wandered over lunch, spent more hours on a phone, drove home. All the while lost in thought of distant places, distant purposes.

Henry David Thoreau in Walden captures the essence of what I was feeling. In Walden, Thoreau's man was too caught up in his own work, his own labors to truly enjoy what life really had to offer. To Thoreau, our chase for material and unessential goals making us less a man, more a machine, unable to truly cope with nature when confronted by it, unable to truly enjoy the greater fruits in life. Most important, our chase in life yielding us little in the way of honor.

Have I found integrity at the wheel of the *Bon Accord*? Was the only real satisfaction I was to enjoy in life prior to that moment I arrived home from work, those moments I spent with my family?

Are my pursuits no longer deemed valid in this day and age? Does one have to have a "career" to feel worthy later in life? Is it even our "career" that we pursue, one of our choosing or is it more a "career" our peers deem worthy of us that we pursue? Has insecurity so crept its way into our basic needs that we confuse it with other needs, give it a place at the table rather than sweep it under the rug?

I know as I stand at the wheel of the *Bon Accord*, I don't scribble on a notepad dreaming of the high seas. I know as I work on her, I don't watch time. I know as I cast off her lines, I anticipate the challenge of each day, and look forward to the voyage.

Sure, the fear of not making a living is real, the thought of not being able to support my family of concern. Yet, they seem distant, as if in pursuing a genuine purpose my needs will care for themselves. The question is, are my pursuits genuine? To some, it may appear a life of leisure, to others merely a boyhood fantasy. What in us decides whether our pursuits are genuine or fantasy? Do we base our choice on the bias of others? Follow a path best perceived by our peers? Have we imposed this burden on the orcas? Do the orcas breach to meet our expectations? Forego their pursuits in life to please us?

In our eyes, perhaps their pursuits involve no more than a king salmon. Yet, what of the orcas' world? Do they live in fear, in constant search of prey, in pursuit of life-sustaining source?

Is it the faint hint of fear that makes one feel alive? I had fear while in a suit—fear of not making my numbers, not closing a sale, not making a paycheck. Though I felt no more alive than I do after a night of too many margaritas. Had the previous twelve years in a suit dulled my senses to an inhuman existence?

Thoreau went to the woods, had I gone to the sea to live a more purposeful life, embark upon a truthful voyage of discovery, see what life had to offer, to learn of myself what to date I had failed to find in a suit?

Have I chosen the path down which the *Bon Accord* was to lead me because I wish to live deliberately? Or at least as deliberately a life as one could lead in this day and age.

As a romantic of sorts, I like the thought. But with three daughters, a beautiful wife, and a loving Lab, I am not going to live too deliberately. I need to maintain a somewhat responsible life, the one that my peers and others know of me, the one my family seemingly questions at every turn. Will my pursuits in life, genuine or not, meet my basic needs?

Perhaps I seek balance in the *Bon Accord* or perhaps it's because I want my children to live their lives not in pursuit of amusement, but in pursuit of life. I want them to taste the finer fruits; I've uprooted them, changed their lives.

It's been one year since I purchased the *Bon Accord* and moved my family to the San Juan archipelago. Am I a different person? To my wife, probably little has changed, other than my wardrobe. Gone are the suits and slick shoes, hopefully here to stay are the faded jeans and T-shirts. To my kids, yes, I believe they sense an easiness in me at times, one absent years prior when I was lost in the world of consumption, hell-bent on keeping up with the Joneses.

I feel my kids' smiles now. In the past I noted them, delighted in them, but never really felt them. Maybe it's the salt air, or maybe it's some spiritual existence the *Bon Accord* is leading me into, but whatever the reason, it's welcome.

I spend a lot of time in thought, up till now I rarely share these thoughts with my wife for fear of appearing somewhat unstable. Thoughts about little more than nothing, halfhearted daydreams, thoughts about life. At the root of it, nature in the San Juan Islands.

A fallen tree, a particular sweep of a branch or shape of a rock, wind-driven waves—it goes on and on, each provoking within me some emotional quality I have yet to qualify. Just recently I witnessed a spectacular scene at the wheel.

It was a clear day when we left the dock. As we headed east along Orcas Island, the cloud formations intensified out of nowhere.

This is rare in the Northwest in that our systems are usually visible well in advance off to the southwest. But in this case, the sky darkened quickly and rain followed, rain that soon turned to small hail as we headed south around Shaw Island.

At that brief moment the sun was out, low on the horizon. The water was glass, smoothed over, not a ripple or wave in sight. The hail hit the glassy surface and bounced or at the very least appeared to bounce.

Millions of tiny marbles bouncing on a glass surface, not with a thud or smack that one would anticipate, but a gentle almost rolling motion. The effect of each bit of hail that fell was negligible as if each that penetrated the water canceled out the ripple of the one that preceded it, maintaining the glassy appearance on the water. Just above the water, not more than two or three feet, rested a layer of moisture, foglike in appearance, as if framing the spectacle at hand.

It was short-lived, soon followed by an encore: a rainbow off the starboard bow. It was magical, as if the *Bon Accord* was floating on a sea of marbles, lost in another world.

There are other moments like this, ones that awe your senses, awake your imagination. At times it's weather-related, at times it is the wildlife; when one is fortunate enough to witness both at the same time, it's awesome.

To see orcas drive off wind-driven waves, their powerful dorsal fins in a sea of whitecaps. To see an eagle proudly perched or soaring against a blackening storm-lit sky, or a harbor seal tactfully balanced on a small delicate rock pinnacle while a powerful storm surge hammers at the door.

Being lost in these moments, one finds contentment, the heart seems to slow, and life seems to go still. The *Bon Accord*, as if on cue, seems to quiet in appreciation, as do most, if not all, of the guests onboard.

Utopia, if a paycheck rests in there somewhere.

I often reflect on these moments at home, quietly drifting back into a dreamlike state. Would my wife welcome these thoughts? Probably not, as all too often they interfere with my chores at home.

She comes from a traditional background—work hard, plant the seeds, and enjoy the fruits of your labor in retirement.

So, I nibble on my fruit along the way, and in doing so, look to discover alternative ways to grow my seeds, and care for my family. In a world where consumption prevails, will our fruits be safe from the pursuits of others? Might we spend years nurturing our fruit only to have it plucked off our plate? What of the orcas—are they safe from the pursuits of other living creatures, namely man?

Over the past year, I've taken the *Bon Accord* on more than 180 tours, each one unique in its own way. At first, I met my peers at the dock and entertained them along the way. As time passed, the tours took on a different appearance. Had I lost myself, no longer a peer with others? Had the *Bon Accord* altered my sense of value, of friendship? Sure, I could still talk a good game, recount a good score, offer insight from another time in my life; but at the root of it all, I lost passion in this voice.

More and more, my thoughts went from those of entertainment to that of questioning. As I sat at the wheel, peering out at the orcas, my focus went from amusement to inquiry. I searched for questions, longed for answers. What brought me to this place? I more and more felt for the orcas and wanted to understand their world. More importantly, I wanted to understand how we've come to prey on their world.

Going forward, I'm relieved the season has ended; summer has come and gone, and we're decorating the house for Halloween. For a brief moment I'm concentrating on ghouls and goblins, not orcas. It is short-lived; I wonder how

I'll bring myself to offer the orcas up for amusement next summer. As I write this, my convictions seem to grow. This scares me—I need to protect my basic needs, feed and house my family. I need income! On an island where tourism, construction, and real estate employ nearly everyone, how will we make it?

I've come up with a new rack card this past week, a four-by-nine inch card that promotes *Bon Accord* Tours. In so doing, I may have penned what some would consider bold language for next season.

"Welcome to *Bon Accord* Tours! We're unique, our motivation sincere. We seek to educate, not to guide. We lead low impact tours, and we promote environmental conservation on each and every venue...To those who come for a 'quick see' of the whales, we say go elsewhere. For those looking to learn about the orcas and the islands, we say book *Bon Accord*!"

Will I put people off? Offend their sense of value, the right to seek amusement while on vacation? To me, it glosses over the truth - most come to these islands for a "quick see" of the whales. For the first part of the season, I sold a "quick see" of the whales.

Next season, what will I sell? What do I need to sell so as to make my pursuits in life genuine? Who am I to say that a "quick see" of the whales is not genuine?

So, I guess I'm traveling all points of the compass in my head these days, searching for bearing and direction in life. The *Bon Accord*, a medium through which to reflect. The orcas are living objects for me to lead a parallel existence with.

I'm convinced my fate is tied to theirs, as is man's fate. Not in their survival, for it seems they'll not perish, but just how they will survive. Will we pursue them to ends of the earth, to those places early charts warned of—places with evil—"here be dragons"?

What a great time to live, in those early days when one could afford an imagination. One was allowed to dream of such places, places with dragons.

Question is, who are the dragons today? Perhaps these early charts foretold our fate. Warned us not to pursue the far reaches, tried to save our imagination, yet our thirst for knowledge prevailed—our thirst to know all, be all, conquer all.

Sure we can look to space, but in most of us there is no hope of traveling to these places. We can look to the deep, too, but with little chance of travel. Has our reliance on technology squashed our imagination, directed our energy toward amusement, a see-all thirst before we go? If this is the case, I'd rather my children not memorize life's puzzles before trying to figure out the pieces.

I want off the ship; how can I persuade others? To justify my pursuits, I need to authenticate them in my mind as well as in others' minds. After all, I am as insecure as the next when it comes to life's chase.

So we sail a sea less traveled, in search of Orcinus orca, in search of a genuine pursuit in life. Hoping perhaps that the pursuit of one will unveil the other.

Friday Harbor

Friday Harbor, Washington, is crescent shaped with a small, inhabited island (Brown) in the middle. She faces east, welcoming the early morning sun, her seashore flanked by a rising shoreline, remnants of a onetime working fishing village scattered among odd-shaped but humble buildings.

It's on unusual story how Friday Harbor came about, and like many of the island stories, it is contested by another. One such tale claims that "Friday Harbor" was an accident. A Hawaiian sheepherder yelled out "Friday" when questioned by a survey boat about what bay this was, thinking the officer had really asked, "What day is this?"

Another story, more often believed to be the truth, states the harbor was named for a Kanaka, named Joseph Pa'ilie, whom the Hudson Bay Company had brought to the islands to herd sheep. Joseph was known as Joe Friday. He grazed his sheep around the soon-to-be Friday Harbor; smoke was often seen from his place and used to steer by boatmen. So it became Joe Friday's Harbor, later shortened to Friday Harbor.

Friday Harbor appears a tad under two miles in length, stretching north/south and no more than a half-mile wide at the entrance. The town itself is tucked in nicely, shielded from most points of the compass. From the water only the first few blocks are visible above the pier, around the northern half of the harbor, as is the activity in town.

From a foot off the *Bon Accord* to land it's about 200 yards along a weathered pier to a little small grassy patch, which is Friday Harbor's best spot for a picnic—a place to sit and soak up the atmosphere and listen to a handful of island musicians that park here in the warmer months, a lively lot with a wide variety of libations. Behind the park, a sloping landscape nestled with berry bushes rises gently upward to the Whale Museum, one of Friday's more vibrant remnants of time past—a two-story weathered pitched-roof house-like building that peers out over the harbor. A colorful mural of orcas graces its facade. Inside, everything is whales, from museum to theater to bookstore.

It's no more than 100 yards along the waterfront to main (Spring) street for those who don't wish to venture the hundred or so stair steps to the museum. Spring St. runs perpendicular to the water, beginning with a roundabout park at the water's edge, just off the Washington state ferry terminal.

The town, or at least the first few blocks, embraces the atmosphere. From nearly every street corner one may catch a glimpse of the water, sit, and enjoy the bustle of a onetime fishing center. In a lot of ways it's a picture-perfect harbor—a page in a Richard Scary book or the harbor you'd find Waldo eating an ice cream cone at a park bench—seaplanes buzzing overhead, steeply descending just off the breakwater, Washington state ferries arcing around Brown Island. An endless stream of private yachts coming and going, some holding fast at anchor, U.S. customs officers parading up and down the pier, inspecting each vessel upon return from points north. An occasional bald eagle soaring over en route to Point Caution, momentarily circling over the University of Washington marine labs to the north end of the harbor.

The town, or at least the postcard version, is an odd collection of buildings and tourist trades. There are glimpses of her past just across from the Whale Museum in Friday's Historic Inn, a Victorian-era hotel that belies her age. The Front Street Café just off the ferry terminal continues this theme in proud fashion in steamed eggs. Another curio of sorts, Funk and Junk offers relics of old. Inside are bits and pieces of island history, nautical and otherwise, that tell of her past. One finds black-and-white photos, bronze portholes, period furniture, utensils, and other odds and ends. It's one of those places you can spend a day in, not shopping, but learning by way of your imagination, creating the past in your mind through objects, not readings. Others, like the Cannery restaurant that sits on stilts precariously overlooking the boats, best sandwich in town here; a Sunken Park, Roy's latte stand, a Crab House, Tommy's Pizza; and my family's favorite, the little ice cream store along the waterfront. Each adds to the character of Friday Harbor, some more than others; each makes Friday Harbor what it is: a quaint seaside village, a onetime working harbor, a remote outpost in the far reaches of the Northwest, home to and frequent stopover for some of the most beautiful wooden boats in the world.

A Sea Less Traveled

The climate in the northwest corner of the United States makes an ideal environment for boats of wood; relatively low humidity, stable temperatures, and salt water add to their longevity.

Large oceangoing schooners, converted fishing trawlers, outdated tugboats, and small pocket cruisers, each unique, and each with its own story, rest in Friday Harbor from time to time.

One particular boat moored next to the *Bon Accord* is a fantail launch built in 1920, *Scamper*. She has plied the inland waters here since her birth and her owner boasts that for every coat of varnish and oil applied over the years, there is equal part brandy splashed on her cabin sole. Her owner, resembles her in many ways.

The *Scamper* is thirty-six feet long and nary a fathom in width. She carriers a fantail to stern, a round sweeping aft section that graces her lines and speaks of her period. From her stern going forward, there is a small aft section or cockpit that leads up to her cabin door. Her cabin house spreads her width as it progresses up to a small, yet formidable by design, pilothouse. Her bow is pointed with steep angles urging along a graceful sheer-line back to her fantail stern. She proudly wears "1920" on her flanks. Like the *Bon Accord*, her lines speak of a period when boats were designed by artists and gentlemen, not financiers and banks.

Perhaps wooden boat owners become their obsessions over the years like many say a dog takes on the personality of its owner? While she is largely intact, a few blisters here and there tell of the *Scamper*'s age. Her bronze fastenings leak a small trail of rust through her freshly painted planks; her bright work, while mostly finished, shows patches of neglect here and there—no more than any other boat, just hints of age, those hard-to-reach spots that escape inspection while onboard. She is without peer on the docks in terms of her age, most of her kind long neglected, and lost to firewood.

The retired schoolteacher who frequents her door shows the same wear—a crack in his glasses, a hitch in his giddap. Both have aged well—perhaps a product of their relationship over the years? And both seem to enjoy each other's company, only going out on occasion, both happy to have one in each other's company, sitting in the slip, soaking in what each has to offer.

Will I take on the personality of the *Bon Accord*? A steady resolve to meet life head-on and leave as little a wake in passing? I could fare worse.

The *Bon Accord* rests in M6, main dock, just down from Friday Harbor Fish Market; a small barge nestled in at the foot of the pier, best fresh fish in the Northwest. Scattered about her are a collection of boats from different times. A handful of commercial gill-netters or purse seiners sit in their slips to starboard, dreaming of days gone by.

To port, two classic old boats, eagerly at bay awaiting admirers, a chance to chase the tennis ball. Off the *Bon Accord*'s bow rests the *Western Prince*, a forty-foot onetime charter fishing boat from Gray's Harbor along the Washington Coast, now turned whale watch boat.

The rest of the harbor is littered with small cuddy cabin cruisers, small barges, sailboats, a few other whale watch boats, and every make and model of power cruiser. There are pockets of charm, boats worthy of reflection: a Hinckley picnic launch, a number of canoe stern cruising sailboats, and a few odds and ends here and there.

I need look no further than three slips down to find another fine example of William Garden's work in a thirty-foot-plus schooner, *Rainbird*. Like the *Bon Accord*, she sits stoically in her slip like an aging lab on her master's porch—proud, unwavering in her affection for all that pass, shining brightly for those she knows appreciate her evolution from the mind of a great naval architect.

Rainbird, it is rumored, William Garden designed and built for his honeymoon. In looking at her detail, the care and craftsmanship that went into her, perhaps he spoke his lust for his bride-to-be through *Rainbird*? What was he thinking as his pencil touched the paper? What was in his mind? This is the essence of a true wooden boat: designed and built, not only to serve a trade, but as a celebration of life.

What was he thinking when he penciled the *Bon Accord*? Is it my place in life to write what I hope is not her final chapter, but a continuation of her proud past?

Other examples of his work and other master boat builders enter the Friday Harbor from time to time, each beautifully maintained and equally operated with care. Each boat has its own personality and life's story. I often wonder how I befell such a fortunate position as to be able to witness these works of art on a daily basis, always taking two minutes in silence to enjoy their lines. Of course, there are a few that require more than two minutes, but after all, boats are my trade, right?

The *Adventuress*, a hundred-foot schooner that arrives weekly as part of a sailing foundation of some sort, bedevils the eye in maintenance calculations. From her planks to her cabin top, from her decks to her spar, she's all wood and proud of it. This next year, I hope to board her and learn of what's below.

It's not always the big ships; every so often a small, less than forty-foot sailboat or motor yacht will enter the harbor, steal my thoughts, and redirect my energies toward their lines. It's not necessarily the prettiest or those with the most gleam in their finish. It's the boats with a story, a past. Like *Rainbird* and *Scamper*, the ones with human involvement I search for, most just happen to be wood.

They come in slowly, without fanfare, quietly approaching the breakwater searching for a spot to tie up. The right spot, not too big—these boats don't take up two spots. These boats seem to slide into just the right amount of dock space. They are handled with care, even the unsightly crafts. I'm not sure what draws me to these boats—retired salmon trollers, tugs, odds and ends. Two of my favorites sit just over the Fish Market from the *Bon Accord*, the *Urania* and the *Stingray*, one a fifty-five-foot-long retired fish packer, the other a salmon troller. They are both of wood construction, weathered beyond reasonable care, but still afloat, still with a story to tell. The hulls are both black and white, thick, heavily built. Their pilothouses are well designed, curved and proportioned just so. Paint hasn't been applied in years; old lines sit in their holds. They could probably be had for a dime, but I wouldn't trade them for any of those bars of soap that litter the pier on a busy weekend. On one, the troller, a rather expensive stainless-steel barbeque rests on her deck next to a lounge chair, perhaps foretelling of her fate.

The above boats are the type I passed in my youth, stopped to observe, and longed to someday captain. In truth, I wanted to be a tugboat captain. These boats, like the old tugs, reek of sweat and stain, their appearance as unsightly to some as a long forgotten woodshed. Yet to me, they speak volumes about Friday Harbor, about our pursuits in life. They are treasures to Friday Harbor, albeit their fate is probably tenuous at best. I can only hope a few younger ones pass by and learn of themselves, "I want to be captain of one of these boats someday."

I often make the mistake of trying to impart the same enthusiasms for these craft to my passengers for the day. Most look at me with amusement, inside mulling over the thought of spending the next four hours with a somewhat unstable person. It is about this time I like to tell people, "I moved here from Kansas a few months back—never been on a boat before, had a premonition, had to go with it, used to be a dentist. What is that noise?"

Like many small boat harbors, all the pleasing sounds, smells, and feels are present in Friday Harbor. What of the *Bon Accord*? Does she feel the thick morning air, heavily laden with salt and moisture from the marine night? Does she listen to the dancing halyards from her wind-driven counterparts?

I know she revels in the early hours each day. All is quiet in the morning air. Aside from the squawk of a gull or occasional great blue heron that has been scared off its perch, things are still and at peace on the water.

All the noises that make a harbor romantic are noticeable: creaking planks, clanking halyards, even the smallest of ripples felt on the water, heard bouncing off her hull. This is the *Bon Accord*'s time to reflect on her world, time for her to soak in her environment.

The air is thick; a blanket of mist rests on the boats as if in-difference to the coming day. The water is glass, reflecting the faintest of images. Through the mist, a backdrop of evergreens, firs, and cedars can be seen over on Brown Island and a slight hint of a wooden troller can be made out off on a distant anchor, the red and white of a crab pot marker ever so slightly bobbing in the foreground. Not much else comes into view—not much else needs to come into view.

On days when I'm privileged to awake from within the *Bon Accord*, nestled up among her planks, seeking warmth from her timbers, I feel the same heightened senses, the simple pleasures inherent in silence, in taking things in. It's a peaceful existence for me, or as close as I'll ever come to one. Is it through the *Bon Accord* I feel this existence? I wish the same for the orcas, moments like this, quiet moments, free from noise.

It's short-lived, soon replaced by the sounds, sights, and smells of a onetime working harbor. Seaplanes buzzing in just off the breakwater, which flanks the piers, plastic wheels on oversized luggage struggling over each and every weathered plank on the dock, krchunk, krchunk. This ensuing rush, is this what the orcas experience each morning as forty boats circle in? What goes through their minds at first morning light?

The bullhorn on the ferry advising everyone, "Welcome to Friday Harbor." Engines cranking over, revving, smoking, dying off to faint idles. People, bikes, kayaks, marching, marching, marching in pursuit of that "magical" feeling, the one all too soon forgotten onboard the *Bon Accord*.

For fifteen years now, the *Bon Accord* has sat at M6. She has witnessed an untold number of boats come and go, passengers walk by, seen changes in the harbor, seen the havoc a northeaster brings down from Canada, yet she sits in silence. Does she, too, float in silence, like most of us in life seeking only to protect what is ours? For want of not appearing a fool, shielded by insecurities, biases toward others, or fears as to how our peers perceive us?

Perhaps she is biding her time, awaiting a worthy mate. So, she rests in Friday Harbor, sizing me up, learning my fears and my passions in life. I too hers, learning her intentions, seeking her knowledge. What is to come of this relationship, perhaps the islands will unravel in time just what part of her life's story I am to tell.

For Charter

Charter boat captain. It's not the exact title I envisioned out of college, or graduate school, for that matter. I prefer just captain, and in truth, the thought of operating a boat for a living as a fisherman or tugboat skipper had more appeal or at least a more romantic vision to it when I was growing up. I always liked the rock star status "solo-around-the-world sailors" enjoyed as well.

My work is good, though, challenging as it may be, it's a sea less traveled by most. Picking up one's family and moving to a remote corner of the country in search of whales, buying an aging wooden boat, and living on an island. I see my family's perspective. To them, perhaps we're seeking to avoid responsibility, avoid growing up and the pressures that go along with life. In their eyes, I might appear a little nuts. But what if in pursuing a more simple life, we find a peaceful existence, one absent the worry and pressures. It's a life I enjoy, one my family will seemingly forever question—but after all, I'm only thirty-eight, not your typical semi-retired professional who has sent his children off to college and beyond and is now looking to live large on an island.

It's been over a year; we've embarked on our second winter. Tours have slowed to a crawl and, sure, pressure mounts on the finances. In October, our net income was $2,000 in tours. Ouch.

Over the last year, we grossed no more than $40,000 in tour sales, those seeking this lifestyle be warned. Hardly a windfall of income and nearly half of my previous take. Plus, over 80 percent of this income comes in June through September.

Our peak season rates are $59 per child under twelve and $74 per adult. Group rates for four or more average $49 per person. Being a six-pac boat—a designation so awarded by the U.S. Coast Guard for I am only allowed to carry six passengers—on a given day my maximum income is approximately $440 per sailing.

Costs to run the charter business are few, but even so, a steady stream.

Basic Yearly Costs

Fuel	$5,000
Moorage	$4,000
Maintenance	$2,000 (low estimate)
Insurance	$2,000
Telephones	$1,400

So we struggle, netting no more than $25,000 this past year. Yet, at the same time, we feel we accumulated more wealth than ever before. Will this romantic vision endure a few more years of net $25,000? Not sure I'd bet on it; the odds seem against us. Nonetheless, we feel it's worth the risks, the rewards worthy.

One of the difficulties in a seasonal tourist trade is that income is received over the better part of six months, May though October. This is the same time of year that relatives visit and long lost friends come to stay. We party more and we spend more—two habits we seem to have brought with us from a previous life, both affording us little in terms of savings.

To alleviate our financial strain, my wife works four hours a day at a local bakery, up at 5:00 A.M., home by 10:30 A.M. It works well for the handoff with the kids, and I'm home by 5:00 P.M. most days. So, there's plenty of quality time at home together. I'm certain, beyond a doubt, my wife is, in the end, the champion of our cause. Not once has she questioned our decision to move to the islands to buy an aging wooden boat. In truth, we've thrown our schooling out the window, sacrificed our tenures, and created about as much uncertainty as one can to grow our relationship and to provide our kids with an unparalleled learning. To this end, I owe her a great deal of gratitude.

As for the job description, charter boat captain, I'm not sure exactly how it would read. The qualities one needs are probably best summed up below:

Patience—no room for error here, tested daily, but it's not like you don't have all the time in the world, anyway—you are a charter boat captain!

Sense of humor—a must (preferably dry); your crew is on vacation, and the ability to make them laugh parlays into tips—tips are good!

Ability to communicate—conversation is key to making a long tour short. What do you have in common with a ballet dancer from San Francisco, a chef from Paris, a clown from Russia, and a sniveling four-year-old from Texas? Find out or the tours will get you!

There are two camps that board the *Bon Accord*: adults and children. With very few exceptions, one tends to leave the other to me to care for, and it's not always the camp you'd think.

Kids under six seem to focus their attention inward on a boat—they climb around inside, push buttons, pull drawers, and test anything else that might have a surprise at the other end. Children over six focus outward, their gaze on the sea looking for marine life, for other boats. It's the first group I tease with a genie that hides in the forepeak of the boat. If disturbed, a genie that awakes with such fury so as to rock the boat over. It works maybe one out of ten times—they will not open another drawer.

While I welcome all, I really enjoy the older children for their sense of adventure; they're longing to learn. There's an opportunity here, an opportunity to educate or to enlighten. I saw the transition with my eldest, and with close to 90 percent accuracy I can pin down a child's focus before they set foot on the boat.

The older children inspect the *Bon Accord* from stem to stern, look over her with approval and sometimes reservation. By and large, they look forward to the adventure and seem to calculate the value. They're not driven by the thought of a photograph or an up close encounter with orcas.

The younger children look right into the windows, peering in with a hopeful gaze. In a day they've been awakened at dawn, driven for hours in a rental car, toted across a ferry, and walked a few hundred feet to my door. They are, without exception, in a rare mood by the time they set foot on the *Bon Accord*.

I like to set some sea rules right off with this group, so I position an obstacle in their path—a bright orange U.S. Coast Guard life jacket—right in the cockpit, not two feet from the cabin door. With the younger kids, this is where the sense of humor comes into play. Parents have various means motivating young ones to put on the life vest. Calling it a "boat coat" seems to be more and more the norm.

I'm not sure I like this approach to coaxing. Children have such respect for coats, leaving them behind daily, bringing home Johnny's or Suzy's in place of their own. To me, it lessens the importance in their minds, accessorizes the object at hand. And you're always setting yourself up for the response you don't want to hear, "It's a life jacket, Mom."

I respect those parents that say, "Put on the life jacket," and stand there in front of their child with no sign of cracking or bending to their will. "If you don't put it on, I'll put it on for you." Works fifty percent of the time.

The next line I like to hear is, "We're not leaving the dock until you put that life jacket on." I'd guess nine out of ten times we're under way with this one. As for the other ten times, not sure, I've usually advanced to the pilothouse.

This is where patience pays dividends. I think the record crying airtime over a life jacket is only eleven minutes. For most, as soon as we're under way, their focus changes. Unfortunately, it's usually directed toward food and play in no particular order.

It's during this period on the boat, usually about half to one hour into the voyage, that I've come to dread the word "cheese." Not the cheese that comes on a plate with crackers and an apple in the form of Brie or Swiss, but the word "Cheese" written across a plastic bag, shortly followed by "Puffs" or "Swirls" or any other manner of processed finger food cheese snack. There is no place for these youthful tidbits on a boat.

A four-year-old boy needs only three handfuls of cheese puffs to completely encase his fingers, hands, mouth, and clothes with tiny orange particles of processed cheese. Now, for a boy armed with a belly full of puffs and no mom or dad in sight, it's free rein on all things boat.

And then there are those three out of ten times the child rips open the bag in such fury that 99 percent of the "puffs" or "swirls" empty on the cabin sole. Mixed with a little salt water or fruit flavored drink…a lethal combination.

Perhaps it's the fact that drawers and cabinets are small on a boat, kid-size by nature. Bunks and settees are playful in appearance. Whatever the reason, not thirty minutes out of the harbor, I'm swimming in greasy orange particles with a faint hint of aged processed cheese filling the cabin. To this end, I believe 90 percent of motion sickness may be attributed to cheese puffs.

Like the cheese puffs, other manner of food items all seem to revolve around snacks. What happened to a good old turkey sandwich? In order, my not-so-favorites: peanut butter spread on anything including my upholstery; Pringles, surely innocent enough in appearance, but given to a five-year-old, it's crumb city; popcorn, and it comes in cheese flavor, too!

For Charter

Along with the snacks, parents seem to associate big plastic cups with boating. They usually come in red or blue, sometimes opalescent shades. It's hard not to notice them in the grocery bag, towering over the bags of cheese puffs, nestled in amongst thirty-two ounces of soda pop, as they board the boat.

I'm not sure if it is the creaking shrill sound they make when kids step on them or the little dink sound and ensuing dribble when they are tipped over, or the fact that the more you fill them the more top-heavy they become, but somehow they always seem to get under my skin. Ten of them will fill the entire trash bag under the sink if they're not stacked.

Perhaps it's the fact that kids have little fingers. Like me palming a basketball, it was never meant to be. Yet, those cups board the *Bon Accord* with consistency. One's ability to laugh yields some relief here.

So, what is perfect fare on a boat? Without a doubt, pretzels and water. Low in sugar, light on crumbs, no utensils needed, no cheese involved. For those seeking some more nutrition, an apple works best.

For most of the summer, I provided a seafood platter. Fresh cracked Dungeness crab, local prawns, smoked salmon, crackers and a crab dip: tasty morsels from the deep. Most enjoyed the food, and it provided a good opportunity to educate people on local marine life. I abruptly ended the crab feed upon learning that 90 percent of all allergic reactions to food comes from shellfish. Visions crossed my mind: mom and dad in convulsions on the back deck, children playfully coloring in the cabin, and the *Bon Accord* one hour from any assistance. Think under pressure or, in my case, lose the shellfish.

Ability to communicate has always been a challenge for me. On the *Bon Accord*, there is a comfort zone, one I'm at ease in. Perhaps because it's my world now, and those that board the *Bon Accord* sense my comfort in them being onboard.

I enjoy teaching about all things related to boats and the sea, about the orcas and other wildlife in the islands. I enjoy the guests more and more with each tour. I learn more about the world and myself. I enjoy learning about others' pursuits, their hobbies, especially those that mirror my passion for wooden boats. Most sense my enthusiasm and enjoy relating a story in kind. In turn, I question why they don't follow their pursuits in life to earn a living. Most think I am a wing nut for trying, but admire the goal. I feel their principles, much like mine in the past, are more grounded.

Geographically, over 50 percent of my tours come from Wisconsin and Texas. The rest come from every corner of the globe. In a span of one month, I entertained onboard the *Bon Accord*: a ballet dancer from San Francisco, a juggler from a French circus, a chef from Paris, a couple from Zimbabwe, a colorful lot from Russia, and a student from London. Over the year, if memory serves, over twelve different countries were represented on the *Bon Accord*.

One of my favorites and, oddly enough, a very polite group turned out to be a punk rock band from Europe, which will go unnamed so as to limit the potential impact of my endorsement on their record sales. This band traveled like rock stars as well, flying in two minutes before the tour on a seaplane. Equally impressive, it took them about the same amount of time to devour my seafood platter that day. I'm pretty sure they took the meat out of the shells? In all seriousness, it was a good day on the water—four hours of very dry humor, coupled with seeing a grown man in a Mohawk actually become somewhat teary eyed at the sight of the orcas. The rockers talked a good game—tough shell and likeable inside—but when it came to wildlife, they showed as much youthful enthusiasm as any, the orcas eliciting within them that "giddy" feeling, the emotion more and more appear to be overwhelmed by.

I've seen it in an elderly woman of mid-seventies, as she raced up through the cabin screaming, "This is the best day of my life! It's amazing!" I've witnessed untold numbers of younger girls in their preteens become ecstatic at the sight of the orcas swimming in unison, breaching off in the distance. In this youthful group, the orcas sense the young girl's excitement, too. On more than a few occasions this past summer, orcas appeared to roll over and glance at an ecstatic young girl. I'm not sure if it was the pitch in her excitement or the pop in her eyeballs, but whatever the effect, it was certainly cause for the orcas to take notice.

There were other days, ones I wish ended no sooner than they had started. There was the twelve-year-old kid with excruciatingly bad breath who drilled me all day with question after question no more than ten inches from my face. There was the blustery day with five-foot seas and an older guy telling me twenty minutes into the tour he had an angioplasty two weeks prior. Once a man asked me before the trip if we'd chum the waters for the orcas for him? And there is the occasional child that pierces your ears. Having three daughters, I thought I'd heard it all. Not so. On one particular day I thought the paint was going to peel off the V-berth walls it was so loud.

These tours are few and far between. For the most part, they are enjoyable. Most importantly, they teach, help me learn. I like what I do and love doing it.

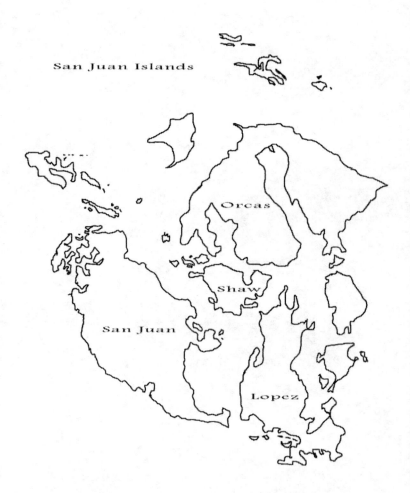

San Juan Islands

Magical yes, spiritual maybe, for the *Bon Accord* the San Juan Islands are home. In Friday Harbor she resides, approximately twenty minutes over the water to her birthplace, Turtleback Mountain on Orcas Island. Although in her current form, reincarnation may be a better description. After all, she was born a seedling, a hundred or more years ago, felled by man for his pursuits.

The San Juans are a collection of islands, some big and some small, most inhabited, a few—those fortunate enough to fall under the NWR (National Wildlife Refuge) status—left untouched. All total, some say there are over five hundred islands. Most of these are only visible at low tide and include all manner of reefs, rocks, and islands. Of these, only a hundred and fifty or so are named.

The *Bon Accord*, in Friday Harbor, is on the east side of San Juan Island, in the middle, facing Shaw Island. To her southeast is Lopez Island and to her northeast is Orcas Island. The waterways in between these islands are San Juan

Channel, Upright Channel, Wasp Passage, and others, varying in width from one-fourth of a mile to one mile and maybe more in the wider passages of San Juan Channel. Combined, these four islands make up more than two thirds of the archipelago's landmass, and are home to more than 90 percent of her population. Between, in, and around them you'll find the rest of the five hundred or so reefs, rocks, and islands.

The *Bon Accord* has traversed the inner waters; she knows the rocky shores, the tree-lined banks, and the sandy spits. From the water, they often appear as one, blending one by one into a sea of evergreens, firs, and cedars, interrupted slightly by the withering skin of a Pacific madrone, an orangish-red tint at the foot of her forests.

From her shores to peaks the archipelago rises gracefully on the largest islands—Orcas, San Juan, and Lopez. She doesn't soar like her volcanic neighbors, Mount Baker and others off to the east in the distance, nor blot the sky with sharp peaks like the Olympic Mountains to the southwest.

The San Juans can best be described as soft. Even the sharpest of rocks appear content in their surroundings, offering not the slightest hint of aggression. Perhaps a sign of her age are the graceful and proud mountain peaks from a once glorious Asiatic plate, slowly receding into the waters that surround her. Rather than challenge the sharp peaks and boisterous volcanoes to her east, she seeks to impart her patience on them, teaching her wisdom to a new continent. The islands reflect this calmness, this peaceful existence. Each island in its own way creates and adds to this existence.

Orcas Island, from the water, appears a green sea of soft mountains and valleys extending upward to her peaks; Mount

Constitution and Turtleback Mountain rise sharply off her northern shores, the taller (Mount Constitution) to around 2400 feet above sea level. She is an odd shape, a badly disfigured hand of sorts reaching out to the other islands. Two waterways, East and West Sound, reach up into her palm, her fingers stretched out and around offering scenic vistas from nearly every point along her shores. She is equal to San Juan Island in mass, one square mile larger I'm told, yet appears double in size by nature of her shape with her elongated fingers, far reaching sounds, and rising mountaintops. She is a dramatic island.

According to David Richardson in his book Magic Islands, Orcas Island is believed to be named after Rivella Gigedo de Orcasitas, viceroy of Mexico, who sponsored the Spaniard Francisco Eliza's expedition to the islands. It is also believed Orcas Island was named after the whales the Spaniards encountered off the northern side of the islands, which are called "orcas" in Spanish.

The book Magic Islands offers an historical account of the San Juans, and comes highly recommended on the *Bon Accord* during tours. The book is short and sweet, readable in a ferry ride, and it contains bits and pieces of island history and lore, unlike most of the other island reads that tell you how to spend your money.

A smaller island, Lopez appears a soft shell by comparison, barely reaching a few hundred feet from the sea. Her southern flanks are craggy, rocky, at first appearance forbidding, but upon inspection a safe haven of sorts, one within which to seek shelter from a strong southerly. Mackaye Harbor, a onetime fishing center, rests in here, hidden by the small islands that continue up her eastern shore as if in orbit around her core. It is this side of Lopez that greets most of the oncoming storms, not indifference, but as if holding a hand out, welcoming, not warning. The small islands and rocks off her southern tip are littered with shorebirds and graced by seals year-round and sea lions in the winter months. These small islands are rockier in appearance than those found elsewhere in the islands; their trees have retreated, pushed by the relentless southerlies that harden her shore. Along the western half of Lopez, a sandy bluff gives way to a sandy spit, which in turn opens up to a scenic bay (Fisherman's). Boats drift aimlessly at anchor in the calm glassy waters within this secluded bay. It's a quiet island. Her northern shores, the ones that face Shaw and Orcas, mirror their neighbors: quiet tree-lined banks, heavily forested in spots, interrupted by an occasional rock outcropping.

Shaw Island is at the heart of it all, positioned snug within the archipelago, surrounded by Orcas to the north, Lopez to the south, and San Juan to the west. To her east, the waters open a little, and off in the distance is Blakely Island. Shaw is the one island that appears from the water to offer symmetry in traveling the length of her shore, hints of sandy beaches in secluded coves, quiet bays from which to seek solitude, and dense forested banks that seem to hide her interior well enough to the naked eye. It's a mysterious island.

San Juan Island seems to encompass a little of each island: soft peaks rising in her northern interior, sandy bluffs along her southern beaches, and rolling hills, quiet bays, and inlets flank her northern coast.

To compare each to the others is a bit futile. The islands feel like one, not like separate islands; they seem to go hand in hand with one another. San Juan without Orcas would just be another island. Lopez without Shaw would be just another place. As a whole, they make up the San Juan archipelago. A perfect balance exists here, a magical existence not found anywhere else in the world. A quiet peaceful aura fueled by the moon tides, churning waters, and endless summers.

A day in the islands is unlike any other day.

At dawn, the islands awake with a gentle ease: colors amassing from the early hues, different shades reflecting off the calm waters, picking up the brownish tints in the rockweed, sea cabbage, and bull kelp that dot the shoreline.

In the winter months, a number of berry bushes lend contrast to winter's gray; goose, elder, huckle, salmon, and serviceberry all grow well some of the more moist pockets around the islands' shores, as do dogwoods and crabapple. These shrubs offer some of the most brilliant shades of auburn or red in their stalks. Another, the soopolallie, or buffaloberry, has a spotted copper color to its twigs. In the summer months, each offers a white to red berry of sorts.

I've never been one to notice shrubs or a twig in the past, not sure the reason why they catch my gaze from the *Bon Accord*. It could be the long winter months, those that offer endless shades of gray, that create a thirst for color. Or perhaps the sea of green that rolls on and on atop the sloping shoreline. Whatever the reason, I like what I see from the *Bon Accord*.

These reddish tints seem to part by the noon hours. Mostly, on sunny days, the color is replaced by blues and greens as the sun rises higher in the sky, lighting the mass of evergreens that stand proud over her reaches and the deep blue beneath the *Bon Accord*.

It seems to be ever changing from the wheel of the *Bon Accord*, heightened more in the winter by the low arc of the sun over the islands' shores, shades of gray picking up the pink in the granite, the red in the madrone and alder and cedar trees, and the tints noted above. Even the sea color is always changing from a deep grayish blue to emerald green to frothy gray in the winter storms.

If there is one point in the day I seem to appreciate more than others onboard the *Bon Accord*, it's that point when the sun's arc has reached a certain angle on the water's surface, lowered itself, and shifted its gaze to the horizon, leaving the water behind to one of the most beautiful shades of blue you can imagine. It's a maroon blue, a deep, dark, mysterious shade that mesmerizes this captain, and adds depth to the canvas at hand. And when a slight breeze lifts a ripple into the sea's surface, creating an endless sea of tiny shadows against the ripple, it's my Eden of sorts. Even the lapping of water against the *Bon Accord*'s hull seems to slow to a rhythmic trance, leaving you spellbound at the wheel.

There are constants too in the islands, perhaps the *Bon Accord* deemed me worthy of or badly in search of discovering. From her cabin, patience is learned, life's pace slowed. To see wildlife in the San Juans is magical: to see a harbor seal balanced upon a rock for hours on end, or to see an eagle perched on the same branch for what at one time seemed like eternity. Are these the lessons one learns in the San Juans? They warrant thought, make you slow and appreciate what you are fortunate enough to be a part of, and bring contentment to a hurried soul.

San Juan Islands

A seal looks for no bigger a rock than is needed to rest, an eagle no bigger a branch from which to peer. What in us drives us to seek bigger rocks and better branches?

If there is another constant in the islands and perhaps another lesson, there is no straight path between two points. To go from one point in the islands to another is never as a crow flies. It's not uncommon to travel all points of the compass each day, ducking the flood tide or seeking an ebb tide with which to gain an advantage en route. The view is always changing at the wheel, with each side of the islands offering equally beautiful shoreline and wildlife.

The northern side of the archipelago has more coastline and more islands, all dotted with even smaller islands and rocks, each magical in their own way. Stretching from Turn Point on Stuart Island (the most northwest point in the islands) to Point Lawrence on the east side of Orcas Island, at eight knots it's two hours minimum to cover the fifteen nautical miles or so of coastline along Boundary Pass and President Channel. In sailing this course from Stuart Island to Point Lawrence, in an easterly direction, one leaves a few islands to the north or port—Patos, Sucia, and Matia—and others to the south or starboard—Stuart, Johns, Waldron, Flatop and Orcas Islands.

Farther to the north across Boundary Pass are the Canadian Islands of Saturna and the Penders, North and South. These islands, along with many others across the border, the bulk of which lie northwest of Turn Point, make up what is referred to as the Gulf Islands, which stretch from Saturna to the east to Vancouver Island to the west—Salt Spring and Galiano, to name a couple. Like other island stories, the border between the two has its twists.

The German chancellor in the mid-1800s arbitrated the boundary line between Canada and the U.S. over a dispute between the English and Americans who co-occupied the islands at the time. An American settler took exception to a pig that had eaten his potato plants, and shot the pig on site. The pig belonged to an English settler. In short, both sides sent soldiers to occupy the island over the dispute, agreeing on a small number of men each so as not to escalate matters too far. In the end, it was left to the chancellor to set the boundary, in which he awarded San Juan Island to the Americans. The confrontation is recognized as the "Pig War."

The northern sides of the San Juans are unique to the islands. Well, the right spots are, at least. In the summer one can find solitude here, glimpses of winter quiet. Migrating birds mingle with harbor seals, sea lions frequent Green Point on Spieden Island during the shoulder season, spring and fall. Eagles soar in the lifts off some of the southern facing grassy knolls. The water is calm, protected from the southerly breezes.

The water is a different shade in these islands, more green, more pure. It is in these waters the *Bon Accord* seeks solace from Spieden Channel, a heavily traveled thoroughfare that lies just north of San Juan Island outside of Roche Harbor. It is in these islands one learns patience; one comes to appreciate the beauty of the islands. Not for their grandeur or locale, but for their simplicity, the balance that exists. To see a pair of nesting eagles perched just above a small rock outcropping littered with seal pups is humbling. To see flocks upon flocks of migrating birds circle above pools of bait fish just off a bed of bull kelp, is inspiring. All the while, aggressive rip curls churning the waters, lifting nutrients toward the surface, sustaining life for those that live above.

At other times when the waters are still, it is as if the *Bon Accord* has awoken me to a tour of the past. I see the islands as they once were from the wheel of a ghost ship, the *Bon Accord*. I see the present daily at her wheel. I've yet to see the entire future through her planks, and to some extent I dread the day she awakens me to this nightmare. I see glimpses on busy weekends, three-day holidays, days the sun shines bright. I've seen a hundred boats chase a pod of less than twenty whales. I've seen boats beach themselves onto the very same rocks a hundred seals make their home, scattering them into the water, putting the fear of God into barely-week-old pups.

It's the days she brings me back in time I look forward to most, offering a magical existence, the same one the islands are so known for.

There are other spots in the islands, those that offer this magical existence. Quiet bays or open shores that offer glimpses of the past, a peaceful balance within view of the *Bon Accord* as she sails past or through. She slows to a crawl; she leaves no wake, only humble appreciation for what these special places have to offer. Turn Island off San Juan, Blind Bay on Shaw, Wasp Passage on a quiet day, the Cactus Islands, President Channel. In comparison to a forty-foot Bayliner doing twenty knots through the same spot, she is but a whisper in the wind.

Along most of the San Juans interior island shores, one finds bays, inlets, coves, each with a few boats at anchor and/or few homes along their shores. A balance seems to still exist, peacefully within these areas. There are others, though: those where too many houses have been jammed in, those where too many boats seek to travel. Balance ceases to exist in these spots, these glimpses into the future. The *Bon Accord*, she travels past, uneasy in her surroundings, eager for relief, for open waters from which to leave these areas behind.

The "west side" of the islands, as it is commonly referred to, offers little shelter in comparison to the north and south, only a False Bay in mocking fashion. One less than six inches in depth, yet the perfect anchorage to the naked or untrained eye.

The waves and wind are stronger on the "west side," which stretches nearly the length of the archipelago on up to the northwest tip of Stuart Island. Between the "west side" and Vancouver Island is Haro Strait, a thoroughfare for steamship traffic from around the globe; ships pass day and night to and from Vancouver, British Columbia.

It is here we often find the orcas, chasing the salmon that frequent her shoreline for the better part of the summer. The salmon enter the Puget Sound area via the Strait of Juan de Fuca. It's hard for salmon returning to their spawning rivers to avoid San Juan Island, and thus it has become a feeding ground for the orcas and other marine life, waters rich in nutrients.

For the *Bon Accord*, it's an hour in favorable tide to reach these spots. It's a different view, looking back at the "west side" from the *Bon Accord* once we've left her behind. The *Bon Accord* often travels off the archipelagos shores a ways out toward Discovery Island off Vancouver Island, bringing the length of the islands into view. From the pilothouse, you see the bare southern stretches, the densely forested north, and soft peaks rising over the island's interior, shielding them from the mainland. Under the *Bon Accord*'s planks, a thousand feet and more of blue water, fathoms and fathoms of rich marine life.

The waters are busy here, boat traffic more businesslike, purposeful: commercial fishers, tugs, freighters, tankers, containerships, and whale watching boats dot the strait. To the west, Victoria on Vancouver Island, British Columbia, lies about eight miles abeam, so known for high tea at the great Empress Hotel.

Lost in these seas is the sense of security. The *Bon Accord* appears small, as if humbled by the big ships, or as if in traveling far from her home she's but a fraction of herself.

Gone is the security the islands provide; shelter in their lee, warmth in their tree-lined coves, she plows on brave. It is in these waters I question my fate and that of the *Bon Accord*, while looking for hard-to-find answers. Perhaps, in viewing the islands from a distance, I realize how relatively small a part we play in their evolution, and, in turn, the evolution of the orcas.

In contrast to her tightly knit interior and expanses along the west side, the eastern flanks of the San Juan Islands are intimidating, rising steeply out of the water on the back side of Mount Constitution and Blakely Island, offering little solace in a big wind, with no bays or inlets. They're not as welcoming as her other shores, as if placed so to hide the Eden within. There are cracks in her armor, though, two or three small breaks in her shore, the *Bon Accord* knows them well—on either side of Blakely Island are two small through ways, barely a football field in width.

It's a pleasure to traverse these shores along Rosario Strait, stretching from Point Lawrence up north to Davidson Rock, off the southern tip of Lopez Island to the south. It's a straight shot, points north on the compass. It's mostly untouched canvas: a sea of evergreens rising to proud peaks, their waters fueled by strong tides and powerful breezes. In traveling a stone's throw off the island's shore, I see only evergreens in my gaze, cedars and fir trees. Their heights seemingly go on for ever past the eyebrow on the *Bon Accord*'s cabin top. To peer at their reaches one needs to go outside the cabin, on deck to look up. On the other hand, to stay in the cabin and to imagine their heights or their reaches offers one more beauty in the unknown of it all.

Rosario, too, is heavily traveled, opening up to Georgia Strait to the north, the beginning of which is a wide open passage, past Vancouver to the inside passage. It is a route many seek to travel in the summer months.

To the east are the islands of Cypress, Sinclair, Fidalgo, and Guemes. They are not considered part of the San Juan chain, technically at least. From the wheel of the *Bon Accord* they resemble Blakely and Decatur, their closest San Juan neighbors. Yet they are not named or included in the guides and travel books as such. Just to their east lie the mainland, Anacortes ferry, Bellingham, and points east and south in the U.S.

Weather

Pitter-patter, patter-pitter…ah, the sounds of rain on the roof of the *Bon Accord*. I'm not sure exactly what it is about rain and a boat…love it though. Perhaps, it's in the interpretation. One can't see the clouds from a boat, or at least from the *Bon Accord*, it's hard to view twenty degrees off the horizon from the wheel. So, there is a certain amount of intrigue to the sound above, the sound that goes on and on, no two drops ever sounding alike. Or is that snowflakes?

In any case, the sound is mesmerizing on a boat, especially a wooden boat. The rhythm to it all, the ever changing patterns, the occasional swoosh of water cascading off the awning set up over her boom to protect thee from the very same water she spills out. To the imaginative mind, it's a symphony of ever altering sounds. I believe one hears what they want to hear in rain, at least those that see past the gloom and the gray.

Down below, up in the *Bon Accord*'s V-berth, huddled beneath a blanket of sorts, reading or at the very least appearing to be reading, the rain offers a different depth of sound, depending on which part of her cabin top you seek to hone in on. To drown out the sound immediately above, just over the forward cabin brings into tune another sound of rain over the pilothouse or a different tone farther aft over the settee, each unique.

The thickness varies on the cabin as do the angles and slope at points, each offering its own contribution to the tune at hand. Coupled with a breeze and chop in the sea beneath, it's a musical experience and awesome to be a part of at times. It offers a unique perspective on rain, not the wet that douses you, or ruins your shoes, or fogs your windshield. It equally brings you to appreciate the warmth and protection the *Bon Accord* provides. The essence of a boat is to shield you from the elements, to provide shelter at sea. The *Bon Accord* is impressive in this respect, offering not a hint of moisture on the wettest of nights.

The San Juan Islands are in what is considered a banana belt; the Olympic Mountains to her southwest pull the moisture destined for the San Juans out into her rain forests, leaving a swath of blue skies in their lee. Annual rainfall in the San Juans is somewhere around twenty-six inches, or nearly half of Seattle's rain totals, I'm told. To say it rains nine months out of the year here is misleading. It may rain a day each month out of the nine months, wishful thinking I know, but no more misleading than to say it rains nine months a year.

We lived on another island off Seattle for a few years, and a few years in Seattle, too. Without a doubt, we notice a difference in the weather up in the San Juans, most notably in the fall. It rains less and when it does rain, it doesn't last as long. I'm not sure of the exact weather phenomenon that takes place in a so called "banana belt," but I can attest to the results. In comparison to the Seattle area, there is definitely less moss in the San Juans. This is good.

It's not to say I don't enjoy the rain; I feel the total rainfall in the San Juans is ideal in many ways. It provides water for us, it waters our gardens, and it keeps our air clean of pollen (it tries, anyway). Best of it all, it reflects light.

From the wheel of the *Bon Accord*, one sees the islands through varying shades of gray when it rains. It heightens the colors, brings out the richness in the islands. On sunny days one battles the glare off the water, color fades into the sea of evergreens above. Even the orcas appear more powerful, more mysterious in the gray mist that hovers just above the water when it rains, a slight hint of steam off the forty-eight-degree water.

The rain does have its drawbacks on the charters; the guests will huddle in the pilothouse as it becomes the last remaining dry vantage point, and eventually fog up the windows. Luckily, there is usually a young one who enjoys working a squeegee for the first time. The rain also makes the decks slippery, which makes the captain uneasy.

Overall, though, it's welcome, and in the spring and fall the rain will pass by, providing sun breaks and an eventual rainbow. At times, we catch a rainbow connecting two islands, making for a spectacular sight.

Other days it pours steadily all day long—never the huge drops you see in the South or East where humidity seems to grow the rain in size, but more like a constant drizzle. It's on these days three little wipers work overtime on the *Bon Accord*, whining excessively in rebuttal, to no effect. It's on these days I wish for a little breeze to make the tours a little more exciting for people, a chance to feel the elements, the rawness to it all at sea.

***

Waves over the bow bring a certain amount of fear to some, to others it seems to perk their senses, awake their adventurous side. Like a good cup of coffee, a wave over the bow, especially one that reaches the aft cockpit, invites conversation onboard.

It starts with unassuming questions from the passengers as to the strength and seaworthiness of the *Bon Accord*. Once they feel satisfied in my reasoning, conversation evolves into an experience of sorts, an adventure, and one to write home about.

Of the two-hundred-plus days we've taken the *Bon Accord* on charter, there has only been three days, maybe four, that I had wished for better weather.

Christmas last year, a family of four, two kids and their parents, a couple moving to the islands from the east coast. It started out innocently enough, twelve knots of wind at most. I picked them up over at Deer Harbor on Orcas Island. The plan was to take them out around Spieden Island and back before the weather really hit, about a two-and-a-half hour tour. Not thirty minutes into our voyage, winds rose to twenty-plus knots at about the time we left Jones Island abeam. As we approached Green Point the waves became steeper, whitecaps breaking, but still manageable for the *Bon*

Accord. About ten minutes later, the whitecaps were being blown off the tops of the waves, streaks of grayish white froth streaking down the face of the waves as they grew in size and temperment. Of note, this particular area in the islands is well known for the rip curls, the charts foretell as much. So, it was a little steep for the *Bon Accord*'s guests that day. Luckily, the seas were coming from astern the *Bon Accord*, pushing us down the face in the planing motion mentioned earlier. It wasn't so much of an issue at that time. We soon tucked in behind Spieden Island and sought shelter within her lee while we traveled along her northeastern shore.

The trick was getting back to Deer Harbor once we circled back around Spieden Island to weather. At first, we headed to the north shore of San Juan to find relief from the southeasterly that was hitting us. This worked for a short while, until we reached Limestone Point, a small rock outcropping marking the northeast tip of San Juan Island directly across Spieden Channel from Green Point.

The seas were only five feet, maybe one or two larger on occasion, but not much. It was the distance between them that created the conditions, barely clearing amidships of the *Bon Accord*, fueled in intensity by a two- to three-knot ebb tide. Had I not been barely four months on the wheel and took the time to study the tides that day, I would have seen it coming. The *Bon Accord* managed, taking the seas at twenty degrees off center. I had visions at the wheel, thoughts of my career as a charter boat captain ending no sooner than they had begun.

It ended well—momentous rises off the crests of the waves and desperate free falls into the abyss, water everywhere, kids actually laughing. We turned around once, for a respite, before circling back. Another twenty minutes of uncertainty in my passengers' eyes, and we were seeking shelter around Jones Island.

There was another occasion; the wind was calm when we left Friday Harbor. One hour in, as we cleared Cattle Point, the winds started to grow, whitecaps settling in from the south. I had two onboard—a mother and her daughter. The daughter was proud of the fact she never got seasick, forever giving advice to her mother on how to avoid the same.

She used all the tricks—don't stare at the horizon, take a breath of fresh air, I think she even tried the wristbands. As we reached Lime Kiln Light, midway up the west side of San Juan Island, an ebb tide was running the other way. Within about thirty minutes, the wind picked up out of the south and, fueled by the ebb, the waves grew to about five feet. At about this time, we headed south to parallel J-pod off the coast.

The seas were gentle by comparison to those off Green Point; the *Bon Accord* took them head-on with no worries. Only, the younger of the two women was nowhere to be found. Turns out in talking such a good game, she actually got seasick. I'll never forget the smile on her mom's face as she stood up with me in the pilothouse grinning from ear to ear, while her daughter spent a good half hour doubled over in the head.

A few other times we were caught out in the wind, once with a fellow who just had an angioplasty, another with a group of sisters who were taking their mother for a tour. The latter tour was probably the day with the biggest seas the *Bon Accord* encountered last year. We were two hours into the tour, no sight of orcas, and we were actually headed back in when over the radio came a sighting—a pod of twelve orcas headed north along the west side of San Juan Island.

Again, it was a combination of a southerly picking up and an ebb tide peaking. And we would have seen the whales had the orcas not turned and headed south right in front of us, the orcas swimming seven knots, and the *Bon Accord* traveling maybe seven and a half knots in the same direction. We steamed on, but when the seas picked up to seven feet or so we were going seven and a half knots up and down, not forward. We were not as successful as the orcas in countering the increasing swell that day. This was one of the few days the *Bon Accord* actually felt somewhat weak—perchance the fact she disappeared in the swells made her appear more vulnerable. The trough was wide, though; it wasn't a crash-into-the-next-wave kind of day, it was just the depth of the drop that created that knot in your stomach.

***

Fog, or a cloud that accumulates on the water, mostly comes in the form of bands or layers of heavy mist nearly one hundred feet or so off the water. It moves in from the Strait of Juan de Fuca on days; on others it gives no warning and seems to slither in from either the west or north. For the most part, it seems to appear early fall, around late September or thereabouts, to be consistent.

As the *Bon Accord* heads south through San Juan Channel out toward Cattle Point, we see it off in the distance, stalled just opposite Cattle Point Light. The fog tends to develop a band from the west off Victoria, British Columbia to Cattle Point, and then east on up through Rosario Strait. Some days the fog hovers here until about noon, slowly dispersing, lifting as we approach the light. Every so often, it darts up into San Juan Channel as far north as Friday Harbor. Some days it engulfs the islands. On a few occasions this past fall, we were steaming along at eight knots, heading south toward Cattle Point about the noon hour. Skies were clear, except for a band of fog as noted above. Once we reached Goose Island, the fog intensified, engulfing the *Bon Accord*.

Goose Island is a small, barely half acre in size rock that cormorants and other seabirds seem to favor, the former choosing to nest here in the late summers. It is situated about a fourth mile northeast of Cattle Point Light. While it's an intriguing island, it offers some tricky currents as it sits right in the middle of Cattle Pass, an area known for its strong tides.

On one particular day, we slowed in caution as the visibility was reduced to no more than fifty feet off the bow of the boat. For a brief moment we were moving at four knots into a four-knot current, fifty feet off Goose Island in fifty feet of visibility. Off to starboard, fifty or so cormorants perched quietly on the rocks, about pilothouse level to the *Bon Accord*. It was a brief amount of time we stayed off Goose Island, maybe five minutes, but it seemed like an eternity. Not sure what it is with fog, but it has that quality, that ability to alter time in your mind.

We soon turned back toward Friday Harbor, the fog apparently settling in for the day. It was a good choice. I spent the next hour listening to boats on the VHF trying to spot a false killer whale in restricted visibility, with not much success.

Weather

As we headed north, the fog led us about two hundred yards off our bow, carrying us up the channel in a sea of dense white mist. We had the flood tide behind us so we quickly traveled the seven miles or so back to Turn Island, just off Friday Harbor. The *Bon Accord* does not have a scanner—a virtual map that shows your location—of any sort. She is equipped with radar and GPS. In the islands, though, it's your senses that seem to guide you more than anything. The way the water is flowing, outlines of trees and rocks, noises, seals off Turn Island, or seaplanes circling above. It's not to say I don't use the radar. It's crazy not to when one can't see one hundred feet off the boat.

At times, we stop the engines and listen, not so much in worry or want of location, but just to listen, to hear the sounds of fog. Like the rain heightening the colors, fog seems to heighten sound in the islands. A lone kayak paddling through the mist just off to port, the sound of its hull gliding, paddles entering the water. Through sound in fog, you create an image before you see it. It's magical in a way; it tests your imagination, your interpretation of reality. To hear seabirds squawk and dive, sea lions struggle to lift their enormous bodies out of the water, or the blow of a marine mammal, all in the fog without being able to see the animals, creates almost a better picture in your mind than reality; it lasts longer, too, if you let it work for you. I never sensed this before the *Bon Accord*. I saw fog and cursed it for the most part; it offered delay and frustration, not an awakening of the senses. How do we teach this awakening, bring others to explore their imaginations?

***

Puffy, wispy, billowing, spotty, and big gray mass: not your technical cloud description and true mariners would probably laugh at these images that fill my logbook. Nonetheless, they are more playful than stratus, cumulus, cumulonimbus or cirrus. I'm not a student of weather as much as I should be; I enjoy analyzing the sky, though, seeking to learn or pick up clues from its formations.

From the wheel of the *Bon Accord*, clouds appear just above the horizon on up to twenty degrees through the forward pilothouse windows. Off to starboard, I have a small door I can slide open and stick my head out to glance above if needed.

My favorite formation in the islands, without a doubt, would be the billowy ones. The ones that float low in the sky, barely a few hundred yards off the surface of the sea. I believe this would fall under orographic stratus—moisture laden clouds concentrated around landmasses with sloping wind patterns. Or maybe they're of the cumulus humilis variety—pockets of warm air rising? In either case, these formations are often sitting just off South Beach on San Juan Island and over higher elevations in and around the archipelago. They appear soft, often framing a mountain in the distance or lending a little contrast to the blue sky as a wooden schooner sails by. I've seen these clouds in Monet paintings too, seaside ones mostly, so I know they're favored by others.

The wispy variety we tend to see before the storms, those off to the south high in the sky; I believe these are of the altostratus or cirrostratus variety? They are sometimes transparent, at other times a dense gray. They slowly approach in advance of a front. The days we're out and these clouds are just starting to form, we usually brush them off; precipitation usually follows later in the evening or the next day, well after we've retreated to the harbor for the night. On occasion, they're spotty in nature, uniformly covering a good portion of the sky above the *Bon Accord*. I believe these are altocumulus?

The ones we do fret over, I believe go by stratus, though don't quote me. They seem to approach with a front, large bands of dark gray clouds low on the horizon, within the scope of the *Bon Accord*'s forward windows. At times, blue skies filter in between, offering sun breaks; other times there are no breaks. These clouds usually bring the wind to the table with them, on strong days near forty knots, with gusts over fifty knots along the southern shores of the San Juans, namely off Salmon Bank. These are the days we keep the *Bon Accord* tied up. We often travel down by car to see the waves crashing on the beach. It's not a day for the *Bon Accord*. The relatively shallow waters of Salmon Bank (fifteen to twenty-five feet) provide ample irritation for the waves as they approach from the deep, lifting them up into a frothy rage just off the beach. It's a magical setting —the sun just above the horizon skirting the blanket of gray overhead, a faint hint of a rainbow off in the distance, a cauldron of blue-gray devilish seas as far as one can see in the foreground.

It's easy for us to know when to go down to the beach to witness this work of nature. Our house is such that we sit perched atop a knoll that opens up to False Bay in the direction of most storms. The wind seems to get pinched through False Bay, accelerating right past our house at its peak. As I type this very sentence, thirty-plus knots of wind are swaying a 150-foot fir tree in a precariously wide arc over our house.

***

May through October there is no greener grass in terms of weather in the San Juan Islands. Temperatures are steady in the mid-seventies for three months in the summer, high sixties during the shoulder season—it's ideal. Humidity hovers around 30 to 50 percent on these days, a non-factor for a good part of the year.

Wooden boats thrive in this environment, with no 90 percent humidity to fill their grain with moisture or desert-dry air to shrink their planks. The water temperature is usually around fifty degrees, plus or minus a few. The air temperature varies little above or below, down to low to mid-forties over the winter and up to highs in the seventies to low eighties during the summer. We receive a welcome frost and an occasional snowfall in the winter.

From a maintenance standpoint on the *Bon Accord*, we need highs in the low sixties, at least, to put on a good coat of paint and cross our fingers hoping there is no dew that night. So, painting has a bit of time constraint, with very few windows of opportunity between charters in the warmer months.

On the *Bon Accord*, her enclosed cabin shields the elements well, but what she has in resistance she lacks in retention, namely heat. While her planks are thick and her beams stout, her large windows and old style sliding doors, the one without any foam trim piece, offer little aid in warming the cabin on days when the winds are out of the north. Even the lightest zephyr that sweeps down from Canada will chill you to the bone when the temperatures are in the forties. Over the last winter, a diesel marine stove heated the cabin, providing warmth for the colder days, those below fifty degrees. It burned diesel from a little tank placed in the head, which is a nice application for a working boat—no propane tanks, no alcohol sponges to ignite, just a little diesel out of the tank. This winter I have no such aid; I tossed the stove after a few episodes of frustration on the boat over the summer (when it was seventy plus degrees) and I had reservations about burning a fuel known for its non-healthy effects. In any event, we're hoping for temperatures in the sixties soon. For now, it's layers and more layers, although with each passing season our threshold for cold temperatures seems to be dropping, not quite to the level of a seasoned islander, but getting there. I've become rather fond of wool socks, too, and have discovered that these are by and large the one necessity on the colder days.

In truth I welcome the cold as much as the wind, the fog as much as the rain. From the wheel, each offers its best, as if inspiring within one another a challenge for more. Like the ever changing sounds within the *Bon Accord*, the weather keeps one guessing, keeps one's perspective in life in tune with nature here in the islands. Let it rain!

Islanders

If in true search of an islander in the San Juans, one would be hard-pressed to come up with a description. At thirty-eight, I'm hardly a judge of character and I spend most of my time on or near the water.

I see more than few middle-aged men with beards, more than a few with gray beards. I see a lot of youth on the islands. I see a lot of other people on the islands too, but to say who is a part-timer and who is not, I'm still learning.

The island (San Juan) population triples in the summer months up from around 7,000 to over 20,000. So, there is about a one-in-three shot of finding an "islander" in the summer. You can narrow the search by eliminating most of the folks found within the town's four downtown blocks these months.

There are a number of families that have lived here for generations, others that have moved here recently. To say one is a true islander and the other a fool's islander doesn't fall under island character as far as I can tell. Then again, we're still considered "newbies," a term used to define islanders of short tenure. So, I'm probably not the best person to offer characteristics of a true islander, and I've spent very little time on Orcas, Lopez, and the other islands. I can offer a few observations with a grain of salt, though. If by chance I offend an islander, I offer my apologies.

Islanders share one thought: the beauty that surrounds us all equally humbles us. It's hard to escape. For most of us, our immediate reaction is to protect this wilderness setting, this hard-to-find peaceful existence, and hide it from the rest of the world. Unfortunately, some take it a little too far.

It has impassioned a number of people and in turn a number of organizations. Some would like to see zero growth, some wish to return to the days of the Pig War, and others, and I guess we fall into this category, wish to see it preserved for future generations. At the same time, we want the islands to remain a welcoming place for strangers from around the world, grow diversity and character, but not at the cost of the landscape itself. Groups such as the Friends of the San Juans and the San Juan Preservation Trust are working toward this aim.

Another common thread for islanders, which some confess to, is that many of the islands' inhabitants might best be described as wing nuts, self-described loons of sorts. I mean this in a good way. There are more than a few artists, craftsmen, writers, painters, farmers, and the like, as well as a few of us that like to pose as such. Square pegs trying to fit in round holes elsewhere in the world, having moved to the islands not to fit into square holes, but to quit the game altogether. Seek a life outside of that best perceived by our peers.

Islanders

Once here, the islands grab you, free you of your previous biases in life, create this feeling of genuine comfort within, a restful soul and a desire to do what you really like to do. For me, it's captain a wooden boat. For others, it's drive an old pickup with a shovel across the windshield, spend aimless amounts of time idling about on a sailboat, for some it is to run a bed-and-breakfast, a quaint inn, a restaurant. Whatever the passion, islanders seem to do what they want to do, which is a good thing, and there aren't a lot of people telling you how to do it, which is a better thing.

The question is income for most of us. How do we afford this life, sustain a living in a tourist-driven economy, a seasonal one to boot. Many of us struggle, willing to forsake some of the finer things in life for the opportunity to live in the islands, teach our children to live simply, enjoy life not just its fruit, work two to three jobs, and enjoy it. Once you've tasted this lifestyle, it's hard to go back.

Over time the mainland, or "off island" as it is referred to when one takes the ferry run to Anacortes, seems to grow in time with each voyage, appearing farther and farther away from Friday Harbor. In turn, San Juan Island seems farther and farther away from the reality of everyday life on the mainland.

At times, I feel like the Amish guy in horse and buggy on I-5, cars speeding by, quickly darting in and out of lanes. I can only imagine what an islander of tenure feels. I haven't seen a stoplight in six months, it's foreign to me, the mainland feels foreign, another country. To see my kids stare out the window of the car in Seattle, peer up at the "space noodle" (otherwise known as Space Needle), brings visions of the astronauts peering out at the moon in Apollo 13.

Time travels too fast when "off island." Luckily, the return ferry provides more than an hour to reintroduce oneself, a chance to slow down. It's as if some type of time warp exists or the islands being in some type of perfect balance keep us in tune with our forks, the rest of world struggles, races to find their balance, lest they be struck in the rear by their forks.

Islanders also seem to have a mutual respect for each other. A majority still wave through their windshields, others nod, some smile. Most have the time to lend a helping hand and not ask for anything in return.

Best of all, a smile goes a long way on the islands, and speaks volumes about a person. I'm not sure I would have believed this in my previous lives, but here it seems to connect people. There is very little "jit-jat" so to speak (no pun intended), and no cocktail hour banter, at least outside of the Chamber of Commerce meetings; and no one is afraid to look you in the eye, which in my mind is genuine, no-strings-attached smiling. Conversation is used sparingly, and when used, it's to the point.

If there is a distinguishing difference between those that visit only for weekends and holidays and those that live here year-round, it may very well be something as simple as a facial expression. In an islander, you can sense the year-round nature to their smile, the "I live here through the winter, through the slow time" smile.

In trying to find reasons for the way islanders are, one need look no farther than the islands themselves. There is no one spot that towers above another in what it has to offer. Each tree, each cove, each sandy spit, and each rolling hill needs one or another to create what the islands are about, a unique blend of all these features combined. A large cedar tree is but a tree, but when coupled with a gentle cove, a sandy spit, and layers of fall blooms, it's part of something special. In a way, I think islanders recreate this feeling—each realizes or is humbled into knowing by the beauty that surrounds us that we play only a small part in what makes this a special place. So we tread lightly for not in want of appearing just a tree outside of island landscape.

Over time, some come to treasure this existence, others become unnerved by it. It's a long winter if you've moved to the islands simply to enjoy the island life, the outdoors to it all, the sunny paradise you visited in July. To one who truly seeks to lead a simple way, it becomes a pillar of strength, hardens ones reasons for staying in that it tests your resolve, weeds out those less able to adapt, simplify. Those who perhaps moved here for reasons other than those apparent at the time of their move. Islanders are even keeled, able to weather the long winters' quiet, and solitude, and even come to appreciate them for their beauty.

Islanders learn to forsake a lot of what the mainlanders believe is the norm, forced by and large into accepting less in substance, but creating a more rich and valued life as a whole. Simple things are found on the island: a good two-by-four of lumber, a lone chair by the side of the road, a table on a corner, a basket of canning jars, a blanket with a small hole—these items would be discarded in most places. Islanders welcome the opportunity to create something out of nothing—waste not, want not.

The island kids seem to embrace this theme as well. Spurred along by miles of coastline littered with weathering driftwood, young boys still play adventure, make forts, swing from trees, and build castles. Young girls still frolic in the tide pools, splash in the coastal waters, eager to explore and learn.

The islands' peaks offer trails, the beaches strolls, and the waters exploration by kayak or canoe. These activities are bountiful, malls and such are not.

We've lived in or close to urban areas. The difference we've found is in the attitudes of youth. Those children led around from activity to activity or sport to sport, their days planned from morning until night, become accustomed to the pace, the hectic got-to-do-something lifestyle. When given the opportunity to explore on their own, pillage a beach, or soar down a windy dirt path, they become bored, their imaginations enslaved by a scheduled life, their minds constantly searching ahead for the next activity, the next event. Put them in the forest, they'll sit on a stump with their hands on their face, feeling sorry for themselves. I see them on the *Bon Accord*; some are bored before they even step on the boat.

For youthful islanders, there is no mall or thirty-game, five-state Little League season, followed on the heels of a twenty-game, three-state soccer season. Young islanders are forced to invent, create play, seek adventure on their own, and not wait for an event of some nature to give them a reason to be happy. We play five games of T-ball in the spring and six soccer games in the fall. The kids have the better part of each month in between to play as they like. Sure, boredom forces creativity in the islanders, but at the same time it generates a will to explore, to find alternative means to entertain oneself, which appears more and more to becoming a lost art in youth these days.

I feel a lot of parents recognize this in their kids, wish for more creativity, and book tours in hopes of expanding their interests in life. But I'm not sure you can throw it at them, stick in their face, and say, "Enjoy."

It's just about that point these kids see the orcas and change my perspective. Without exception, the orcas are the coolest thing these kids have ever seen. And for the brief moment we're with the orcas, you can see all the weight in the world lifted from their shoulders and big wide grins come across their faces. It's at that moment they're open to exploration, to learning. It's at that moment I try to instill in them an undying appreciation for the orcas, and challenge them to learn more, while they're experiencing that "giddy" feeling. With most, lines of communication are open for the remainder of the tour, so I see hope in learning.

As far as islanders and the orcas, are we still learning? A hot topic on the island, many different views, each respectful of the others, and each tolerated for the most part. There are some on the islands that wish to see boat traffic cease around the orcas, others who wish to see it curtailed in duration and hours of the day. And others still, although a remote few, who would just as soon see them disappear around salmon fishing season.

The Whale Museum plays a central part in it all, providing a platform for lectures and series on the subject.

It does a wonderful job of balancing the socioeconomic impact of whale watching, conservation, and stewardship, without appearing to step on one another. I'm not sure how they do it.

Whale watching is a hard nut to crack; most of the island's commerce in the summer is derived from same, so islanders with a stake in these businesses are less likely to denounce the trade. For those with no stake, it's just as hard to sift through their motivation; some, perhaps, in thought, believe that if whale watching were to disappear, the crowds in the summer would disappear, a worthy goal for some, ending whale watching would go along way toward this goal.

Others feel since they own property along the coast on the west side that they, in turn, own their view. Whale watching boats are probably an eyesore to these folks, who would like nothing better than an unobstructed view of the orcas off their porch at summer barbeques.

So, each is out to cover their own needs, some more basic than others, and each has a stake in the future of the orcas.

For those of us who don't live on the west side of San Juan, housing on the islands vary, from million-dollar waterfront compounds with very little land to old farmhouses with acreage in the interior valleys of the islands. Most of us live somewhere in between, one- to two-story homes built in the seventies and eighties during a growth peak on the islands, others in small developments scattered about around the island between farms and parks. Rolling hills provide views, if not of the water, at least of the country, for most. A lot of houses do enjoy vistas of the different channels and passes.

Friday Harbor still maintains remnants of her past with a few blocks of old Victorian houses, doing well to keep their spirits alive; setting them aside in a historical society is underway. Around her perimeter, scattered about the few business parks, a few subdivisions appear. The town itself is roughly ten square blocks of single-family housing and a small mix of apartments, again appearing to have been built up in the seventies, for the most part.

Every so often, as you travel the interior of San Juan Island, in and out of the community roads, one comes across something distinctly unique to island life.

Westcott Bay is a prime example. A sign indicates a turn off Roche Harbor Road, a busy throughway that connects Friday Harbor to Roche Harbor. About a mile down, past a collection of houses perched overlooking the bay, a collection of very weathered, leaning walled, sloping roofed, shingled cottages appears—hints of the past, with fishing gear, nests, traps, and the like spewed about in haphazard fashion all around. Green grass and weeds advancing on used paths; overgrown limbs and vines outline the doorways and peaked roofs. Boat parts and some assemblage of boats are visible in the tall grass. It's a windy dirt road, the kind two well-worn narrow wheel width dirt sections run through, leading you to something. The kind of road that tells you you're going the right direction, even though you have no idea where you are going. At the end of the road, a pier of one hundred yards or so emerges, along with a lean-to of sorts—both of weathered wood, darkened over the years and spotted with geese and gull droppings, thus the lean-to. Oyster shells are everywhere, spewed about along the pier, the beaches, and the low-bank waterfront. A number of pot markers or floats are scattered about the bay just off the pier. A collection of buckets rests in stalls under the lean-to. You've arrived—Westcott Bay Seafarms, world renowned for their European flats and other mollusks.

There's no sign telling you where to park or instructions or details on the oysters; just an old scale with oversized dial, akin to that in a meat market, sits next to the buckets of oysters, clams, and mussels. A few slick old rubber gloves and a brush assist in assorting your take and an office around the corner in one of those old weathered buildings takes your money.

This place and others on the island reflect islanders in many ways: no fanfare, just a bare-bones simple lifestyle, and a way to make a living. The oysters bring the business, not a fancy sign, not a colorful building with pretty flower baskets out front, just a few raw oysters plucked out of the water.

There are other local businesses, ones islanders pour their time and effort into, put their stake in. There is a lavender farm, Pelindaba. It offers more products made from lavender than you can shake a stick at. Teas, candles, spices, brooms, even a swatch of twigs that you stick in a pond to keep that sponge green stuff from growing, to name a few. It flowers on and on, as do the fields of the farm, a sea of purple in the summer.

There are a handful of others with local charm, but the ones I find most to island character are the ones that sit out at the end of a drive—a small table, a stump, a bowl, or basket. A sign that reads or tells of where to put our money usually accompanies them. They contain flowers, birdhouses, various arts and crafts, and sometimes feed and farm products like eggs. It's not so much the quality of the product, but the thought that trust goes a long way on the island.

Community is a rallying cry for a lot of islanders; there is a tremendous sense of community building on the island. Perhaps it takes someone from off-island to recognize the genuine motivation people here have for the cause, for their desire to make it better for their kids. It's reflected in a number of events, whether it's in theater or arts or recreation. Islanders seem to have a thirst for community.

The children seem to come first on the island. It's evidenced in the quality of the school system, from the condition of the schools to the teachers. There is an exceptional lot here for those of us who seek this lifestyle. Diversity in education is also prevalent; there are a number of home-schooled youth.

In coaching these youths, I've learned of their character and their dispositions. Maybe it's the islands themselves, but the kids have a certain calmness here that seems to stem from confidence. Not an overwhelming ego type of confidence, but a humble inner confidence. Kids smile more, and they look you in the eye in the islands. It's not to say they're not kids, sure some have a hard time with island life, but overall it's a good group of youth.

Wildlife, Less Orcas

The orcas are, undeniably, the symbol of the San Juans; they are on every letterhead, coffee mug, T-shirt, and postcard. Yet, what of the bald eagles, the harbor seals and porpoises, the sea lions, the cormorants, the numerous migratory birds that travel through…what of these creatures?

Equally powerful to the orcas in many ways, these birds, marine mammals, and pinnipeds are all a part of the San Juans and are every bit as special and integral to the region as are the orcas.

From the wheel of the *Bon Accord*, we see hundreds of harbor seals in a given day, heads popping up to port and starboard, giving a quick glance, sizing up the *Bon Accord*, slowly turning and going under. From one hundred yards they mirror an aging retriever from the water up, one struggling to find his stick in the ripple, two eyes bulging out of a head about the size of a cantaloupe, preceded by a short muzzle with a little snout on the tip. They appear neither scared nor alarmed by the boat, only slightly curious as to who is passing by. Their eyes are mysterious, dark, black holes of intrigue, peering at you as if through you at times. They're a hard read and to decipher their body language requires some creativity. For the most part, they seem preoccupied, forever looking, slightly shifting their gaze from one movement to the next. Out of water they offer not a clue, staring straight, body stiff, balanced precariously on a rock no bigger than a fist. Every so often the water and rock become one, the seal perched atop the water in perfect symmetry, his or her reflection in balance on the glassy surface.

In the winter, they're not to be confused with the sea lions that pass along San Juan Channel en route to and from Green Point on Spieden Island and Whale Rocks just off Cattle Point on the south end of the island.

The Stellar, or northern, sea lions arrive early to mid fall, sometime in late September, and appear during the winter and early spring. They first show up on the south end of San Juan Island, huddled on Whale Rocks at low tide, seeking restful days of sun after their long journey south from Alaska where they spend their summer months. Another large pinniped, the elephant seal, is spotted from time to time.

At up to three thousand pounds, the northern sea lions are a sight to ponder, elevating their massive heads, giving slight grunts and moans, swaying back and forth trying to gain leverage on the rocks to move higher and higher up the rocky shore, to appear bigger than the next. They are a shade lighter in appearance, a tan brown, in comparison to the gray of the seals. In the water, they move slowly on the surface as if treading water and struggling to do so, their noses barely breaking the water, a rhythmic up and down, gentle flowing wake behind. In truth, they are as graceful as the whales in their ability to turn and spin and accelerate with ease. We just don't see a lot of that from the *Bon Accord*. We dare not close within one hundred yards; they're a shy lot, staying down for long minutes, swimming deep, popping up a mile off. At times, they log in unison, drifting carelessly on the surface, resting, waiting for another run at the salmon, birds of flight hovering over.

One of which, a seabird common to this area and one often found on whale rocks with the sea lions, the cormorant (double-crested and pelagic), in many ways typifies islanders. They ask for little in life: a tiny crack in the rocks with which to nest, a small rock or log above the water from which to dry their oil-less wings, and few fish with which to survive and feed on. They are quiet by nature, especially in light of the gulls they share the rock with. They're neither brightly colored, nor oddly distinguishable in any way. The cormorant is a black duck with a long neck and wings, as described by my passengers. They hover low as if in stealth mode in flight, barely a foot off the water to gain lift. They know their weakness and they know their place in the world, neither of which they complain about.

Seabirds pass through, during different seasons of the year. The arctic tern, delicate in flight, symphonic in movement, and peaceful on the water, offers stark contrast to some of the gulls that pass, less one: the Bonaparte's gull, with its striking black head and tailing edges to its wings. These gulls seem dainty by comparison to the more common Glaucous Winged gulls we see off the *Bon Accord* and along the pier. These gulls show little fear. I have to say, in the islands the gulls seem more a part of the landscape than a nuisance. They don't appear to scavenge or wait around for food scraps like in other harbors and ports around the western half of the States. Perhaps another sign of the balance that exists here in the islands, even the gulls are at peace.

Other seabirds we come across, lost in name to this captain, later found in readings on the subject: marbled murrelets, guillemots, and an occasional shearwater. One very elusive bird, and one we have yet to encounter on my days at sea, is the great tufted puffin. We hear reports, sparingly, of one or two being sighted over the summer. I went to the marine park in Seattle just to find out what they look like outside of a reference book, even eat the cereal of name in hopes of forming an attraction for the puffin to the *Bon Accord*, but no such luck. I've missed a few others, too. With each, though, my appreciation for seabirds and the like grows. They provide a welcome diversion, a chance to take one's eyes off the water's pull, shift your gaze just above, and follow the different wing beats and rhythmic flights as they circle the *Bon Accord*. There is always something to see out the window from where I stand with my hand at the wheel; I'm never at a loss for nature in the islands.

Raptors circle the sky above the *Bon Accord* daily, their wings stretched mightily through the sun's rays, as they purposefully stalk the waters and islands below. The bald eagle, golden eagle, turkey vulture, osprey, hawk, and falcon, although the latter two seem to prefer inland grounds, reside in the islands.

Spieden Island, just north of San Juan, used to be a gaming island. I believe it was even called "Safari Island" at one point. Some wing nut, who took the title a little too far, imported exotic game to this tiny stretch of an island no more than three miles long and a half mile wide at its girth. Guests would stay in tents and shoot the animals with little effort, taking the prize home the following day.

While the shooting has stopped, the animals —sika deer and three varieties of fallon deer, mouflon sheep, rams, and other non-predator game still remain. To keep the herds healthy, there is a certain amount of carnage at times as numbers are slimmed, along the west side in the late winter.

We'll traverse this shore, and it's not uncommon to see more than a dozen or two eagles and other raptors perched on limbs just above the water, providing ample photo opportunities for those onboard. It's a bit surreal, especially under a dark sky, stuff a Hitchcock movie would be made out of, but it is an awesome sight to see these creatures en masse.

Other times, we see the bald eagles in flight, just above or off the bow, passing in travel about one hundred feet off the water. Every so often, one will circle just off the boat, hesitate briefly, and then plunge its talons into the sea and pull out a bait fish (herring or smelt) of sorts just abeam of the *Bon Accord* as if on cue. Like the salmon in the teeth of a seal or sea lion, it's a powerful moment, and humbling in turn.

Porpoises frequent the island waters—the Dall's porpoise are often found in Haro Strait and occasionally along San Juan Channel. The harbor porpoise are seen throughout the islands. One is very playful (Dall's), the other shy by nature. At four to six feet, they pale in size to the orcas, but both are special to those who sight them off the bow.

The Dall's porpoises have become quite an attraction for whale watchers, especially on the orcas' days off, those days they are nowhere to be found around the San Juans. The Dall's enjoy riding the bow wake of boats, often seen jumping or dancing out in front of freighters coming around Turn Point off Stuart Island.

Off the *Bon Accord*'s bow, they swerve back and forth, under the boat, appearing from nowhere in pursuit of a ride. They burst out of the water from time to time, puffing a breath in between dives, occasionally spraying a mist into the air. Their bodies are slick black and white like the orcas, though more subtle. They are considered the fastest of marine mammals, obtaining speeds in excess of thirty knots or thirty five miles per hour. At seven knots along the *Bon Accord*, they are playful, appearing to side over to catch a glimpse of those peering back at them. When the *Bon Accord* sits dead in the water, they circle her, popping up on either side as if in a game of hide-and-seek. Their breath is purposeful, breaking the water with a resounding whoosh from their blowholes, before they calmly swim away. The power in their flukes evident in their bodies, strong in appearance, stealthlike to the flow around them, their tailstock or area just above their flukes is arced, as if providing a fulcrum of sorts to leverage the speed they gain with each move.

The harbor porpoises by comparison are extremely shy; one hundred yards from the boat is too close for these mammals. From the wheel of the *Bon Accord*, I often keep silent about their presence. If I warrant attention to their whereabouts, by the time one glances over, they've dived deep out of sight. In turn, these mammals appear to be unnerved by boats, so the *Bon Accord* and I wish to respect that to some degree, keeping a distance from their intended paths, their locations.

We do see other whales on occasion, namely the minkes. These whales are brown to gray in appearance and are of the baleen variety, their diet consisting mostly of krill. On occasion, they consume small fish and squid, or, among the islands, herring and sand lance. They grow up to thirty feet in length, though the ones we often sight off the *Bon Accord* are slightly less. They tend to frequent an area called Hein Bank, located about three miles south, off the coast of South Beach on San Juan Island. At times, we see the minkes lunging through schools of bait fish, scattering about a collection of gulls gathered overhead. At other times, we see them gently moving north up Haro Strait or through San Juan Channel.

They don't move with the power and grace of the orcas; their movement is more purposeful. They rarely breach off the *Bon Accord*, and other playful activity we see of the orcas is seldom observed in the minkes—spyhopping, lobtailing, and such. The minkes stay underwater for long periods as if only breaking the surface to take a quick breath before retreating below. This makes them somewhat unpredictable, often swimming in a zigzag or in a series of diagonal paths to their destination.

There are other whales in Puget Sound. In late February the gray whales begin their swim north from their breeding lagoons in Mexico to the feeding grounds in the Bering Sea, stopping along the way to feed in Puget Sound. The gray whale can be found off Whidbey Island in the winter months. South of San Juan Island about forty miles, Whidbey offers the gray whales more sandy bottoms, a seafloor they prefer to the rocky shores of the San Juans. Humpback whales also appear from time to time, mostly off the coast of Washington. At one point, they were numerous in Puget

Sound, but sightings are few and far between now, and they are more apt to surface off the southern tip of Vancouver Island near Victoria.

I'm not a "naturalist" by trade, although I'm learning, so the preceding descriptions may fall short in some eyes. My failure may very well be in my belief that we all too often zero in on characteristics and proportions of wildlife and in doing lose vision of the real beauty it offers. Size and weight, number of teeth, while important for research and ultimately conservation, takes away from understanding, lessens the learning in it all to my eyes. I point out these traits in response to questions on the *Bon Accord*, but for the most part I sit in silence until prompted. Numbers create calculations in one's mind, the same mind witnessing these creatures for the first time. Numbers invite comparisons, measurements in life that are all too common for most of us. It is not to say science and research are not useful. On the contrary, the work the Whale Museum and Center for Whale Research are doing is paramount to learning and our education. It's the initial impression, the first memory in seeing the orcas or other wildlife, that I feel becomes diluted with fact from "naturalists." These facts and traits are readily available in print. Why do we so associate learning with a fact or figure? Are our minds not capable of forming a bond with another living creature without learning of size and weight, name, and physical makeup?

Wildlife in the San Juans is as much a part of the landscape as a towering fir or cedar, a berry, a scenic cove or pass. If one looks at the islands as a whole, the landscape as an environment; there is no one marine mammal or bird of a feather that stands out more than another in the islands. We may awe at the striking contrast of the bald eagle feathers or become "giddy" over the breach of the orcas, but this is more a function of our education to date. We're programmed to place things on a pedestal, on stage, for our amusement, the bigger the better.

Perhaps in living the island life, experiencing these things day–by–day, one sees wildlife in a new light?

A Day in the Islands

The morning hours are slow in coming on the San Juans. One needs not a watch or an alarm of any kind if in the mood to live island life to the fullest. I wear one on occasion—rare occasion—if only to remind me that I need to correct the time on it. It's been two months since the clocks were turned back and I still haven't felt the need to change the dial. I'll lose the darn thing for weeks on end, too. Unfortunately, one or two of these days I actually need the thing.

A faint hint of a rooster crowing off in the distance may or may not best one or all of my three daughters to first morning light. Even the rooster tends to sleep in during the summer months in the islands. My wife, on the other hand, is awake cranking up an old Jeep pickup, a 1966 Comanche that my father rebuilt for us, to get to work on time, 5:00 A.M. on most mornings.

The rooster, the Jeep, my daughters, my wife—these are the hour hands on my clock. The minutes aren't worth fretting over. There are hints of time all over the islands; the ferries and seaplanes both arrive and depart just off the breakwater from the *Bon Accord*. A commuter flight lands at the airport as I drive along Cattle Point Road to the port. If I miss the ferry, a mass of bodies longingly looking for directions, or a lack thereof, tells of the time.

The best part about this clock, it's not hanging in front of you on a wall or strapped to your wrist, constantly reminding you what time it is, what time your next event, next venue, next deadline is due. In the islands, you can afford to slow time, set your own tempo. Although perhaps "afford" isn't quite the right word. Being able to afford things and live this lifestyle may be more of a contradiction.

If you need activity or a reminder of time, town is a stone's throw away for most. You may circumnavigate the whole island in forty minutes or so and Friday Harbor rests in the middle.

We live in the southern interior of San Juan Island, about seven miles out of Friday Harbor and the *Bon Accord*. To travel to the boat takes me maybe twelve minutes by truck, thirty minutes by bike. With either mode, it's a pleasant commute. There is not one stoplight on the island. As the day emerges, the mood changes slowly in the islands.

The early hours are quiet in town, a few cars darting about here and there, a huddle of ferry goers around the Doctor's office, a small coffee shop just up from the ferry landing and the only one open these early hours in the day. It's at this hour one may find a sleeping great blue heron a few feet from oneself on the dock, its own clock even amiss on these mornings. It's short lived, step on the next plank—creak—

and these birds awake with about as much grace as my two-year-old, true to their appearance, cranky buggers.

It's about the 10 o'clock hour when town seems to roll over from a somber sleep—more cars, more people. The mid-morning ferry is arriving. A handful of tourists pause at each corner trying to recall where they saw that latte sign the night before. A local with dog in tow purposefully walks through an intersection.

It's about this time I venture toward the boat, rolling down Spring Street in the old truck. And it is for just this occasion I painted "*Bon Accord* Charters" on her doors in hopes of wooing my last few passengers for the day. For some reason it doesn't work. Not sure if it's the fact the truck is pinkish in appearance or that the driver's door doesn't close. Perhaps I ought to rethink this strategy? I don't book a lot of drive-by traffic. I once took a seaplane flight in Alaska and the bush pilot actually had duct taped the passenger door shut. If I recall, this didn't instill me with a whole lot of confidence.

The *Bon Accord* awaits my arrival each day, no doubt with reservation on most, a little after the mid-morning hours, before noon, before the *Island Spirit* docks at the end of the breakwater, letting off a hundred or so passengers.

When I arrive at her slip, the first minutes I fumble for the key to her cabin door, all the while peering over her surfaces, looking for a blemish or chink in her coat that may have opened up over-night as I spill two parts coffee and one part creamer on her topsides. I put her to bed with a check of her surfaces too, always wary of her condition.

My tour for the day will arrive in about thirty minutes if I've guessed right as to the time and if I've received a deposit from them. All too often if I don't receive a deposit, the passengers sleep in, miss the ferry, or drink too much the night before. If I receive a deposit, they show.

In those thirty minutes, I flip on the electronics, bringing the *Bon Accord* to life. Her water pump gurgles, her VHF radio squawks in resistance as I tune her to the weather channels. Another moment of hesitation comes each day as I lift her engine box. I fear the day I open this chasm and see a puddle of dark oil spewed about her holds. Today, she is clean, her oil dipstick healthy, her oil absorbent pads dry. Her V-drive or the point in her propeller shaft just aft, appears to have loosened up a little though. Finally, her coolant level is right.

The next step, another in a series of hesitant moves, is firing up her John Deere. Her batteries are aging, questionable, perhaps in need of replacement, but she fires on command with not a hint of hesitation on her part. Her first few rotations are a little rough, but she settles in at 1100 rpm nicely. I spend the next part hour cleaning her windows, wiping her decks, drying her rails, making her pretty.

At noon, I sit at the wheel, reflecting on yesterday's tour, anticipating the day ahead, listening in on the other boats, their whereabouts, what wildlife they're sighting.

My tours arrive usually on time, a family of four, a group of six, a collection of twos, and occasionally a lone traveler. I take no more than six and am thankful the coast guard limits me so. I'm not one to communicate to the masses. As I peer over the dock to the *Western Prince*, I see dozens loading her stern.

Tours average four and a half hours, just the right amount of time to get to know six people, learn about where they come from, why they are here. Onboard, the first twenty minutes cover introductions, safety, and sanitary issues. Good thing humor is not lost on my passengers here.

1200—Winds calm, seas flat, hint of overcast skies.

Shortly after the noon hour, we set sail, almost due east out the harbor. The *Bon Accord* has yet to reach 170 degrees temperature in her John Deere, so we idle out for twenty minutes, allowing passengers the opportunity to find their spot on the boat and, more importantly, their sea legs for the day.

1230—Harbor seals, about eighteen, resting on rocks off Turn Island, faint breeze from the south picking up, skies wispy.

It's about this time we find out which direction the orcas are heading, which course we need to follow to arrive at their location in about an hour or two. The faster boats don't have this problem, bee lining for the whales. With the *Bon Accord*, strategy is involved, patience rewarded.

If the orcas are somewhere along the west side of San Juan Island, as is common during the summer months, they're usually traveling up the island in a northwesterly direction or down the island in a southeasterly flow. It takes the *Bon Accord* four hours to circumnavigate the island in favorable tides, placing a high degree of importance on which course I choose to travel to the west side of the island. If I head the *Bon Accord* south around the southern tip, Cattle Point, I'm rewarded if the whales are lingering around Eagle Point or False Bay, two distinguishing landmarks on the southern end of San Juan Island, or if they should turn southeasterly from points north.

Conversely, I can spend the better part of the four hours chasing the whales should they choose to flip to a northwestern direction. The *Bon Accord* only does eight knots on a good day; the whales tend to travel anywhere from three to eight knots. Throw in a strong ebb or flood tide, and some days we're only doing two knots across the bottom, looking for whales that are swimming eight knots away from the *Bon Accord*.

Once our course is set, the wheel turned over, my attention usually turns to the guests. The first hour we travel the eastern shores of San Juan Island, leaving Orcas, Shaw, and Lopez Islands to the east, off to port when we head south, and off to starboard with points north.

It's a great first hour as many of the guests get to view the islands for the first time as they should be viewed: from the water. Like the Spanish and English explorers that charted her shores in the past, passengers see the islands in all their magic.

This is the hour I enjoy most on the tours, the one that reconnects me to the *Bon Accord*, gives me the motivation to educate those onboard about life in the islands, the whales, the orcas. I learn of others' pursuits, record their ideas and thoughts in my head, search for parallels in my life to share with them. For the most part, my passengers share a common theme. They all appreciate, or at least while they still have the thought in their mind that they're going to see orcas, the simple beauty of the islands. They come from inland origin and have chosen the San Juans to be close to the sea, the water.

Within the first hour, I know my guests and, with fairly good accuracy, can tell their motivation for the tour. I know when those onboard are dead set on a photo of an orcas' breach. I know which ones will be disappointed with the tour if we fail to come within one hundred yards of the orcas. These people pepper me with questions the first hour: "When are we going to see the whales?" "Where are the whales?" "How many whales will we see today?" "How close will we get to the whales?"

1300—Cormorants restless on Goose Island in freshening breeze out of the south. Stellar sea lion off port bow. Seas one foot in slight flood tide.

The second hour is filled with anticipation as we head around to the west side of San Juan Island. From the north, we slide through Spieden Channel and Mosquito Pass to reach the west side, or from the south we round Cattle Point and traverse along South Beach to Eagle Point. Most days, we find the orcas between Eagle Point and Open Bay, a fourth mile or so off the shore. Other days we find them in Rosario Strait or Boundary Pass.

During this hour, passengers are growing a little weary after more than an hour on the *Bon Accord*, their sea legs not quite up to their potential just yet. Rarely does one get sick onboard, though, and we're grateful for the absence of an ocean swell in the San Juans. The anticipation is growing, and passengers see more and more boats heading toward the orcas, boats with brightly painted "whale watching" signs across their hulls. It is about this time the bolder passengers move to the bow of the *Bon Accord*, braving the wind and the waves at any cost for a chance to see the orcas. Off in the distance a breach, a spyhop can be seen to the trained eye.

1330—Orcas off in the distance—two miles at two o'clock off starboard bow. Wind to seven knots, seas one to two feet, skies clearing.

It is at this point, about an hour and a half into the tour, passengers redirect their energies, fumble for their cameras, their binoculars, and their kids. On most days within a half hour we're "on scene" with the orcas, quietly observing. For me it's a half hour of strategy, a chance to assess which way the orcas are traveling, which way the boats are going, which boats are with which whales, and which whales are with which boats.

Lack of speed is an asset here; it affords me the opportunity to be extra careful to find the right spot to view the orcas without stepping on another boat or, more importantly, the orcas.

1400—With J- pod off Lime Kiln park.

We like to spend no more than thirty minutes with the orcas, to allow more room for others to view. This is a good length of time for the *Bon Accord* and her captain. Some say it is too little, too short. It's usually the ones with a camera who complain. Perhaps time speeds up when viewed through a zoom lens?

It's a half hour of frayed nerves on busy days. Forever scanning the waters for boats and wildlife, positioning the *Bon Accord* here, maneuvering there, trying to stay clear, to avoid close proximity to the other boats and the orcas. We're relieved when the half hour is up, the *Bon Accord* and I; a gentle turn of the wheel as we head for port is one of my favorite moments of the tour.

1430—Left orcas at Edwards Point, wind to twelve knots out of the south, whitecaps visible, ebb tide setting up. Passenger sighted Dall's porpoises off starboard bow three-fourth mile off.

It is all too short a moment, when expectations onboard are not realized. It's approaching the late afternoon hours, naptime for some, and the boat trip is nearly two and a half hours along. For those who truly appreciate what they were fortunate to witness, it's all smiles on the way home, a chance to sit back and relax, enjoy the islands. For those with loftier expectations, ones not met, it's one to one-and-a-half hours to port of brooding, time spent contemplating whether or not they got their money's worth going out on the *Bon Accord* that day.

1500—Approaching Cattle Point Light, winds easing, skies clear.

For me it's one-and-a-half hours of thought on the way home, of wonder, of why and how I came to be doing what I'm doing out on the water. It's a challenge to turn disappointment into appreciation, and most of the time my comments are met with reservation by the passengers. Nonetheless, the *Bon Accord* and I steam on. We try to educate, offer insight on the orcas and their environment, and bring passengers to respect our decision not to get too close.

1530—Seeking relief from ebb along Lopez shore, sighted Stellar again off Whale Rocks en route.

The last half hour of the tour is playful one—even the sternest of passengers seem to enjoy a little dry humor here and there as we head into Friday Harbor, occasionally stopping to pick up my crab pot on the nicer days.

1600—Friday Harbor, wind calm, seas flat.

Once at the dock, all is well; the *Bon Accord* is tied up snug, her engine cooled, her accessories put away for the night. She poses for a few photos, her bow proudly inserted between frames, chin up, eager to please. A few good-byes take place. The *Bon Accord* and I are alone again.

It's a moment to pause, reconnect with her, sense her thoughts on the tour that day. Some days she sits quiet, others she creaks a little, offers hints of exhaustion. Mostly on days I've worked her too hard.

On land, the heat of the day hits late afternoon in the summer, and early evening in the fall and spring. The walk back up to the old truck requires a little more thought; the park is full, docks are busy, lots of lingering going on, lots of people parked or "setup" in front of my destination. The Fish Market provides a welcome relief, a quick stop along the dock to pick up some of the San Juans finest, Dungeness crab.

Early evening, about 6:00 P.M., is ideal on the islands. With crab in hand, I find my drive home is painless, without thought for the most part. And what more could one ask upon returning home than to be greeted by three smiling daughters, each with a bear hug for the captain.

The next few hours are family time on the island. With a smooth refresher in one hand and a crab leg in the other, we sit on the deck, lapping up the environment, the island life. As the sun sets, so do the little ones. For me, it's an hour or two on the e-mail circuit, trying to book tours well into the fall, and another hour trying to answer questions in my head—all things boats, orcas, and human emotion.

Maintenance

What is it that makes work rewarding? Is beauty in the eye of the beholder? Is my appreciation for every grain in the *Bon Accord*'s exposed wood a troubling sign of future obsessions? Have I let her down, when I leave an aging blister in the paint for months on end?

The *Bon Accord* has no cover to hide under, seeks no protection of a covered boathouse or shed, and most importantly whispers not a hint of unhappiness. Yet, why do we become obsessed over her condition?

It's an endless task—months on end of worrying, preparation, writing "to do" lists, losing "to do" lists, and rewriting "to do" lists. It's not for gain, at least mine. Perhaps it's spiritual, taking care of a onetime living medium, preserving its strength, its beauty.

The *Bon Accord* consists of mainly painted surfaces above the waterline, with hints of teak trim along her sheer and rails. At her bow flares out six or seven six-inch wide planks of teak, vertically ascending from the water to her forepeak, her knightly shield—protecting her from an unruly anchor, forty pounds of swinging iron, as well as oncoming seas and anything else thrown at her.

Over the past fourteen years, varnish has hastily been applied to the trim and forward planks, thick and yellow, shielding her grain, giving the wood the appearance of a diluted brown paint. It's not right; she deserves better.

For almost a year now, I've glared out her pilothouse at the peeling edges, the exposed patches of bare teak under the rounded edges of her trim found every few feet throughout her length, along with hints of peeling on her shield—signs of deterioration. Yet, to passersby she sits in all her glory. Perhaps the art in her lines yielding some leeway upon inspection?

Armed with a brand-new heat gun, forty feet of tarp, three or four different colors of masking tape, a couple of foam brushes, teak oil, and three or four scrapers, I was up to the task, eager to taste the fruits of my labor. It's simple in theory. Apply heat to varnish, varnish falls off into tarp, vacuum tarp, enjoy smooth refresher—a vision soon lost.

A few lessons quickly learned: (1) a heat gun is nothing more than a very expensive blow dryer, (2) varnish doesn't fall off, (3) heat travels very slowly through varnish, (4) the smooth refresher is a long way off.

Heat, when applied to the varnished surface, pierces the varnish and attacks from within, bubbling, lifting, cracking the shield from underneath. Is this akin to having your teeth drilled for the *Bon Accord* or is it a spiritual existence, being freed from bondage, from the weight imposed upon her by coat upon coat of a suffocating varnish? Would the orcas feel the same sensation as if the weight of traveling through a hundred boats was lifted?

On a four-inch wide trim piece, heat intense enough to lift varnish travels one inch along its length every two minutes. An eight-inch strip, four-inch in width, takes about fifteen minutes to loosen the varnish on.

It starts slow, the buzz of the heat-gun vibrating in your palm, eyes intensely focused on a small square of surface, heat radiating back into your face, the mid-day sun beating down on your neck.

Heat applied, a minute passes, small rice crispy cracking, small bubbles form, lifting, varnish cracks. Heat moves along, not to lose momentum, traveling heat across surface square inch at a time. Ten minutes pass; remember to breathe, heat to surface.

Thoughts, many, litter the mind on days like this. Sitting there, poised with heat gun, pondering the fate of the orcas, the fate of the *Bon Accord*, my fate. It's one of those moments when the dream state becomes a perception of reality, a deep think is as best one can describe. Biases are lost, time stands still, and even chore at hand seems effortless. It's an odd existence, but true.

Perhaps this is the inner secret to owning a wooden boat, working with a onetime living medium. Or perhaps, in peeling her layers, the *Bon Accord* is allowing me into her world? Is this how the orcas feel when not encumbered by throngs of amusement seekers?

Fifteen minutes pass, slight hint of wood burning. Lost in thought, remember to move heat along surface. Eyes blurred, sweat down forehead, back stiff—where's a scraper, quick before she cools. There is a moment of hesitation with scraper in hand, varnish sitting there like hot caramel, awaiting its fate. At first, I approach her with a calm steady hand, scrape, varnish falls, pace quickens, more varnish falls.

The next phase, equally humbling, is sanding her to remove all remnants of past coats. The thick brownish coat has been removed, but under her grain blends with dirt and suet. Sander plugged in, eighty-grit in hand, vibrating, lifting the faintest of particles into the air, gracefully to tarp below.

This phase is not nearly as spiritual as the last; it's more aggressive, a panic mode—press hard and fast, both hands gripped tightly on sander, moving along surface. The rewards come fast; the *Bon Accord* rejoices and her teak lightens in appreciation.

Six hours of one day, fourteen years of varnish lying on the dock, piled high, offering no remorse. Four-inch wide strip of teak, breathing, inhaling, awakening from a somber sleep, once tucked in tightly by layers upon layers of varnish hastily applied to her over the years. Grain exposed, grain revealed, reward recognized.

And for the exposed wood, what next? There are volumes of research on varnish, on oil, on leaving bare. But what of the *Bon Accord*'s trim?

Why do we seek to protect wood, refuse to allow it room to breathe, soak in its environment? Search for that end-all, be-all coat that will ward off the evil environment? Does leaving wood without protection reveal insecurity within us? Does it expose our chase for that "giddy" feeling? Can we preserve a onetime living thing without chemically altering it? Probably not, but it is worthy of thought. Self included, we're all looking for a "well done" from those who appreciate hard work.

After all, I need to protect the *Bon Accord*'s exposed surfaces for fear of drying and cracking.

I can't bring myself to apply varnish, to impose a burden just lifted. I want her to breathe. Never mind trying to avoid that point-of-no-return with varnish. That point when you've just applied a layer only to have the wind pick up or the boat next to you start sanding or those stressful minutes you pick at a loose fiber from your brush that sits in your fresh coat laughing at you. I'm planning not to varnish for her, the *Bon Accord*?

I want her to take in the morning dew, to feel the splash of salt water upon her. Never mind the thankless amount of sanding that lies ahead with varnishing, days of applying coat after coat, and eventually stripping her free again. I want her to sense the feel of her former glory, when she towered over the forest, felt the breeze in her limbs. After all, it's the only exterior part of her finish that is not coated in epoxy.

Her topsides, from just above the waterline to her rails, are battleship gray, two-part epoxy paint that sells for over seventy-five dollars a gallon. In fair condition, her topsides are not worth further inspection at this time. The day will come, though.

Her decks and cabin tops are a different story, peeled and patched over the last year, scuffed from soles, trodden upon by the endless masses in search of orcas. It's a challenge keeping up a charter boat. Days of good weather, ideal for painting, are often booked on charter. A single day, let alone three in a row, needed for painting are few and far between during the drier months.

More than once, the *Bon Accord* has been approached for charter shortly after a fresh coat of primer has been laid upon her, only to go weeks before a final coat. As such, she enjoys playing me like a fiddle. Just when I feel as though I have her conquered, she opens up a blister in the paint, opens up a cut, a chink in her armor.

I've yet to master the art of keeping her clean of small blemishes. Perhaps it's not meant to be? Perhaps I need to perform her well, before she allows me any satisfaction?

Three spots have been particularly troublesome. One is just forward the pilothouse, wheel side. Three little open slashes in the paint atop the forward cabin cause little blisters in the paint within view of the wheel, daring, laughing at me to try again.

At first, a few minutes of sanding, a quick coat of primer, and a finish coat of epoxy paint lasted one month. Next, ten minutes of sanding, cleaning out the residue followed by two more coats of primer, and a finish coat of epoxy paint lasted three months; getting warmer. Finally, all of the above along with thickened epoxy resin lay in her wounds. Thought I bested her, it lasted two months? Odd part, it worked in other places on her cabin top, those unseen, free from my daily glare. So we prod on, playing the game—what is to come? I fear that once I have mastered these spots, will I lose introspection, become insensitive to the passions I now feel onboard the *Bon Accord*? Or will she keep me in check, humble my aspirations, and lead me to a greater existence, a spiritual one?

And what of her power source, her John Deere 108 horsepower, turbo, water-cooled, six-cylinder workhorse with 8,000 hours on her? Why has she not let me down? I've stretched time on her, allowed her lubrication to thin, her fluids run low, subjected her inner working to higher temperatures in pursuit of that "giddy" feeling. Yet she plugs away, with little to no worries.

Over the past year, she has seen ten oil changes, fifteen different oil filters, ten fuel filters, twenty-five gallons of fresh oil run through her house, two new hoses, a new oil cooler, and in return, she offers no worries . No leaks, no smoke, no pings, no loss in power. She fires up on command.

Only once she has failed me, and with most things on a boat, timing is everything. Not five minutes from her slip, she fired off a warning bell—her temperature was hot. At first I thought I had run her too hard the day before, perhaps her coolant leaked out overnight, or the oil had escaped somehow. But I'd checked her fluids before sailing, as I do on every voyage. Had this happened at the dock, no worries; upon inspection I would have seen the fan belt had come loose—a bolt holding it in place snapped off.

In this instance, however, I sat still in the water directly in the path of the 11:00 A.M. ferry loading the last car. If there is one no-no to boating in the San Juan's, you never want to position yourself in the path of one of Washington's finest. It's an empty feeling, powerless on a powerboat, six paying passengers, each a little less enthusiastic about their boat trip that day.

I was fortunate, though; even avoided the five blasts from the ferry's horn, the one that signals danger and lets everyone in the harbor know to look out toward the water, toward the *Bon Accord*. I had a race car mechanic onboard that day. Twenty minutes tops, he had the engine cover off, belt fixed, and the *Bon Accord* under power.

One year ago, a diesel engine was as foreign as flying to me. I had little working knowledge of engines, let alone diesels. My passion was sailing in previous years. An engine was a means to get off the dock and charge the batteries, little else.

After working on her for a year, this John Deere may be my new best friend or at least as close as a hunk of iron can be. I fret over the *Bon Accord*'s power source daily. At 8,000 hours, it's no spring chicken, and lots of TLC goes into her. At first an oil change was a burden, later a chore, and now a ritual. I actually circle it on the calendar, every one hundred and fifty hours. Armed with new filters and fluids, I board the *Bon Accord*, eager to impart new life into an aging vessel.

The process takes about two hours, depending on where you position your tools. Note to self: every misplaced screwdriver and wrench equals two or three stubbed toes. The *Bon Accord*'s engine is positioned in the aft portion of the cockpit, surrounded by an engine box. To reach her inner workings, ten screws are slipped out of the engine box; each side is then taken away, allowing one access to the oil pan and all else that need be reached for maintenance.

Every conceivable human position is achieved in working down in her holds. For every screw one drops into the bilge, many a muscle is put to work retrieving the same. Having your head below your knees most of the time makes it somewhat less pleasing, but there is nothing like awakening to the smell of bilge water, oil, and wood on a cold day.

The first step to a transfusion for the *Bon Accord*, is hooking up a pump to a hose attached to the oil pan. This particular Deere takes a little less than three gallons of oil, so sucking the old oil out of the engine is the first step. With every pull on the pump, a squirt of hot oil—hot dirty oil—squirts into a bucket. With each progressive squirt, the oil blackens; one hundred fifty hours of engine labor darkens the pail. With each squirt I try to recount the past one hundred fifty hours, reflect on the tours, learn what they had to offer.

It's rewarding oddly enough, sitting there covered in dirty hot oil, back aching, knees frozen. It's an opportunity for me to give back to the *Bon Accord*, fill her anew, let her know my passion for her being runs deep.

Once dry, I replace her fuel and oil filters. A mindless task with one brief moment of fury, that point where you slip off the old oil filter, that point where you hope to catch all the oil that comes with it, but it escapes your reach and covers the block, dripping into the pan below, laughing at you, staring back at you, daring you to try to reach down into the deepest depths of the oil pan.

Armed with new filters, fresh oil is poured back into her inner workings. While her covers are off, her zincs are replaced, too. These are small plugs of metal—zinc—that negate the corrosive powers water has on metal. It's a simple process: drain or shut off water source, unscrew plug and replace zinc, screw plug back in, turn on or refill water in radiator and water intake.

If her John Deere represents her heart, than the *Bon Accord*'s undersides most assuredly represent her spine, her backbone. While out of sight under the seas, it is definitely not out of mind. Every year the *Bon Accord* is raised in a sling for inspection.

I don't look forward to this day, as all her wounds are exposed; every stick and piece of wood that has struck her throughout the year lays claim to a piece of her timber. I feel for her when I pull her into the sling. Like when the nurse tells you to put on a robe and wait in the dressing room for what is to come, the *Bon Accord* humbly enters the sling, awaiting her yearly checkup.

In looking at boats at a yard, I've always liked to see their lines under the water. But more and more I feel for them up on sticks, high and dry, on the hard. The *Bon Accord*'s gaze is always forward, off on the horizon, not down beneath her skins where minions prod her, poke her for defects in her hull, walk about her girth in whisper.

Once on the hard, as it is referred to, the *Bon Accord* is pressure washed of all the slime and suet she's gathered over the year, her planks exposed. At first it's a quick glance, a hurried look. One, two, three dings this year, a quick fix with marine epoxy. There is more, however—a blister in the paint, a bubble, and an unsightly exposure.

Her armor has been cracked, her painted bottom and epoxy undercoat chipped away, leaving bare wood. It's a small wound, but troublesome, about the size of a grapefruit that grows with each chisel move. Nothing a little duct tape, hair dryer, and a few gobs of epoxy can't fix. Note: the duct tape is used to hold the hair dryer under the boat to dry out the wood being fixed, not to patch the hole.

Mixing epoxy is an art. One, as noted prior, this boat owner has yet to master or perform. Seems easy enough: two parts mixed to a simply ratio and left to harden. Plaster in the hole and wait for it to dry before sanding smooth. Perhaps working upside down with epoxy or perhaps my impatience in measuring the mixture accounts for my failure to date? Whatever the reasons, my clothes seem to bear the brunt of my efforts. Nonetheless, her ding is filled after hours of heat dried her planks.

Maintenance

The *Bon Accord* is fixed anew or as close as she can be, filled and painted, ready to be splashed again—her timbers soothed by forty-eight-degree salt water, her bottom sides protected from unwanted inspection, her glare returned to the horizon.

Some say I fret over her condition more than my children's.

Orcinus Orca

At up to twenty thousand pounds in weight and roughly the same length as the *Bon Accord*, adult orcas are a sight to behold from her decks. Their features are inspiring: smooth black-and-white skin, towering dorsal fin up to six feet in height, and a powerful tail fluke. Even more inspiring, and equally humbling, is the power with which they move through the water, up and down with their flukes, purposefully in travel or searching for prey.

Orcas swim up to eight knots and as much as one hundred miles a day, travel in a tight pod (family unit), and display a number of behaviors such as spyhopping, lobtailing, breaching, and slapping. From the decks of the *Bon Accord*, all are amazing to witness.

To see orcas breach, soar out of the water and make a resounding splash, within fifty yards of the boat is a guaranteed tip. To see one swim under the boat is a tip and a referral. At the wheel of the *Bon Accord*, I see my passengers' delight, sense their joy and amusement. It's only human to want to please, right?

After all, is this not the same feeling marine parks zeroed in on in the late 1960s, capturing fifty-plus orcas from the waters off the San Juans? They herded them into coves with explosives, helicopters, and boats while our eyes were trained upon the stars.

Yet in passing I wonder, does anyone on the *Bon Accord* look to understand the orcas' behavior or consider why? Or is simply viewing an act—a breach or spyhop—in and of itself the reason for the tour? To what extent do people look for a relationship between themselves and the orcas? To what extent do people look for a relationship between them and the environment they tread upon?

In the San Juan Islands, three pods frequent the waters for the better part of the summer. L pod is the largest and, as of October 2003, numbers forty-one whales. J and K pods number twenty-two and twenty whales respectively. All total, there are approximately eighty-three orcas or "residents" in the San Juan Islands. It is these whales that we see throughout the summer.

There are other orcas that visit the islands, known as "transients" for their unpredictable routes, which reach over nine hundred miles along the coast; these whales offer scientists, researchers, and whale watchers an alternative culture of sorts. The transients travel in smaller pods—a handful at times—communicate with a different dialect, and consume all manner of marine mammals including other whales, sea lions, and seals. In appearance, they're not as powerful as the residents—smaller dorsal fins and body mass—and their behavior would be considered a bit on the shy side by comparison as they tend to stay underwater longer and travel away from traffic, making viewing less opportunistic.

The biggest distinction between residents and transients are the vocalizations of the two: a series of harmonic whistles and high-pitched calls, dialect, between members of a pod or group. Residents appear more vocal, chatty by nature, using up to fifteen distinct calls to communicate with each other, whereas the transients communicate with anywhere from four to seven calls amongst themselves, mostly after a kill. These sounds or "calls" are used both for communication between the whales and for echolocation, the process of emitting a series of sounds (high energy clicks) through their nasal passages and measuring the distance between the sounds and the echo that returns (picked up in their jaw cavity and transferred to their brain through an oily substance). Toothed whales, orcas included, use echolocation to visualize their environment underwater and to search for prey.

Coupled with the fact that residents and transients never interbreed, researchers are using this vocalization distinction as a basis for classifying the residents as a different species of orcas from the transients. This will aid in qualifying the residents under the Endangered Species Act, setting in motion more regulatory efforts around the resident pods (J, K, L) who stay within about a two-hundred-mile radius of the islands from the latter part of May to early October largely in pursuit of their favorite food, salmon.

A third group of orcas, "offshores," were discovered in the early 1990s, seen mostly off the coast of Vancouver Island and the Queen Charlottes.

Each pod (J, K, L) is unique and special in ways. From the *Bon Accord* we learn which whales dive longer, which travel faster, which whales tend to play more, and which tend to avoid vessel traffic the most. We witness females caring for their young, aggressive males testing their mother's patience and resolve, and older females leading by example.

Over time, one learns to identify a whale by their markings: a saddle patch design, a nick in their fin, or a curve to their dorsal. At first they appear as a unit, hard to distinguish one from another, but over time their markings appear more and more to a trained eye, and for the most part a sampling of their personalities begin to emerge.

In witnessing their behavioral patterns from one trip to the next, it's hard not to feel a bond with the whales. Their behavior mimics our own in so many ways. To look off to port and see a mother protecting her young calf—herding it away from danger, nudging it approvingly toward life, and allowing others in her maternal group to aid in her defense—provokes images of motherhood. To witness astern a bold, stout young male discovering his power, his ability to woo female orcas, feel his instincts, or a spry youth eager to please and learn, playful by nature.

The more one sees, the more one grows in appreciation for the orcas. And for this captain, appreciation for life is nurtured.

How does one create this appreciation in others, encourage them to seek a bond with the orcas? To me, learning is the process of answering your own questions in life. Never let your schooling interfere with your education. To me, life is a question, the answers to which are in life's experiences.

Orcinus Orca

Orcas have a lifespan of fifty to eighty years. Does the fact that of the 134 orcas captured from the wild, 110 are now dead and that the average survival time of these whales was less than six years bother anyone? If I fail to educate, will the *Bon Accord* fail me? I've chosen her lines, her path to learn life's lessons, and I feel a passion to educate.

And what of the native Americans that lived in these parts before our time: the peace-loving Lummi Indians, who sought the islands for their bounty or the Haida Indians from up north who referred to the orcas as Skaana, supernatural chiefs of the underworld? The stories they told and passed on for generations? Are their stories about how close they came to the whales, or are they about the orcas' relationship to the environment, their contribution to sustaining the ecosystems within which we all live?

We know the orcas are warm-blooded, use their lungs to breathe air, give live birth, and the babies use their mother's mammary glands to drink milk. Yet, do we truly understand why one group or pod known as "residents" only eats fish and another known as "transients" eats all manner of marine mammals? Or why "residents" frequent these waters around the San Juan Islands for the better part of seven months each year and why "transients" simply pass in transit to some other place they simply pass in transit? Sure food is the main reason, but maybe there's more?

At first, I longed to please passengers, my eagerness to educate was there, just overwhelmed by greed. I sought high appraisal from those onboard. I felt in viewing the orcas, passengers who had first sought amusement would develop an understanding and seek more knowledge. But where do you draw the line? Where does amusement end and education begin? Perhaps this would be my first lesson on the *Bon Accord*?

I have too much time at the wheel to ponder these questions and most may have already been answered? Yet questions like these onboard the *Bon Accord* seem worthy. A trip absent of any inquiry is just a "boat trip" in my eyes. Is this worthy of the *Bon Accord*? She too wants to educate. She too wants to let people know of the fate of the orcas, of the risks they face from overpopulation, toxins, and lack of salmon.

She comes from felled timber, trees fertilized in some part by the same salmon the orcas need for their survival.

The *Bon Accord* has a relationship with the sea, and in turn the orcas. Have I jeopardized this in taking her out simply for amusement on days when there is no inquiry? I hear noises in the engine, in the hull, and in the rigging that otherwise would be absent, as if she is letting me know her displeasure.

I'm convinced she feels the orcas' pain, hears their cries, and through her fir planks and frames she's going to make me feel them, too.

On some days I feel as though I've put her on a stage, with a sign out front, "CLOSEST TO THE WHALES, $49— CLIMB ONBOARD." She deserves more! It makes me hollow inside when I see the orcas' tail-slap, whap of the water with their fluke, directed at the *Bon Accord*. This is a sign of aggression or warning on the part of the orcas. I've violated their space, jeopardized their relation to the *Bon Accord*, they're letting me know. Though this same behavior elicits cheers from whale watchers?

What must the orcas think? Perhaps it's the same thought caged tigers and lions have when audiences clamor to see them fed, lining up just before, smiling and cheering with each roar? They're protecting their food, warning us not to get close. And at the same time we must see, must get close. It's cruel, yet it's become acceptable to let people into the feeding pens at zoos everywhere, some even publish feeding schedules.

On other days, I make the *Bon Accord* proud; she rolls along in sync with the waves, in tune with her environment. Is it on these days I've proven worthy? I've respected her space, and in turn, the environment she represents? Am I rolling along in sync, too?

Unfortunately, on these days I've not lived up to the expectations of my passengers. I failed to position their lenses for that pivotal shot of an orcas' breach that will make or break their trip. They've come to expect that shot—and why not? Over one hundred flyers and rack cards, Web sites and brochures have that shot; why shouldn't they?

What of the orcas' space? My comfort level is around three feet for strangers. The *Bon Accord*, she likes at least two boat lengths. What of the whales? Is it OK to position a boat in their path? Is it OK to parallel their swim from less than a hundred yards? Many private boaters and whale watch operators alike believe this is OK, sacrificing the personal space of the orcas for five minutes of amusement, all for the greater good of a healthy tip or toast to the captain.

To me the beauty in the orcas is seen from afar, at least a quarter mile off, if not more. To see them swim in a pod, in unison, against a dramatic backdrop like the San Juan Islands. To see them breach, sleep, rest, and log in unison, as a pod or super-pod, is how the orcas should be viewed and no less appreciated.

Perhaps then we can come to understand their relationship with the environment in greater detail, right? We're looking at a beautiful work of nature, magnificent art, and zeroing in on an eye patch, a massive dorsal fin, a powerful fluke—through zoom lenses.

Are we failing to look into the orcas' eyes, feel their pain? Why has evolution camouflaged the eye of the orcas? The easy answer—to confuse their prey—makes sense. Yet, is it the same markings, the black-and-white patterns, that bring us to prey on their space?

What is within us that drives us to be on top of something: up close, must hear, must feel, must be within five feet of the orcas? Is this the net effect of marine parks around the country? We've seen Shamu breach in a plastic tank from twenty yards away, so anything less is unworthy of admission?

Is this the extent of conservation the marine parks have espoused their contribution to over the years? "Hey, they're not 'killers.' Let's play with them." Are the orcas better off now than when they were when ancient mariners coined them as "killer whales"? Would whale watchers seek small inflatable boats and desire to be within an arm's length of the orcas if there was any inclination that thirty razor-sharp teeth might chomp down on them?

Is it wrong to want to answer these questions?

The *Bon Accord* sees it all; she sees expectations across the board. She delights in the innocence of a twelve-year-old girl who sits on her bow, smiling in admiration at the sight of a harbor seal off in the distance, or an eight-year-old boy who grasps her wheel for the first time, grinning from ear to ear as he sets her to the oncoming seas.

Unfortunately, she sees the other side, a life full of unfulfilled expectations. Those that sit in disappointment on her stern, those that failed to get that pivotal shot of the orcas' breach up close, within feet of the boat, or those that have made the trip only to see the orcas and are going home with nothing more than a boat trip. In their minds, they wasted their money and time going out on the *Bon Accord* that day. They failed to get the shot, the magnificent breach of the orcas. Never mind that very few boats were out, the weather and lighting were spectacular, and marine life abounded.

The *Bon Accord* knows I suffer, not from failure to please - from failure to educate, make people appreciate on these days—and she enjoys it, often dumping water she has collected in her awning just over the back cockpit onto my head as I hop off to grab her stern line. Perhaps this is my fate for not discounting their fare. The best line I've heard all year after one of these trips was from another captain: "It makes you think, doesn't it?" The *Bon Accord*, she'll sail again, though, and we'll rise to the occasion.

On one particular trip, seas were flat, skies clear, although there was a slight hint of fog approaching, it was a beautiful day. We steamed down San Juan Channel in a southeasterly direction, leaving Friday Harbor behind. Onboard the *Bon Accord*, we had six passengers. My favorite words were heard from one just leaving the harbor, "It's a beautiful day! If we see the whales—great; if we don't—still great; it's nice to be on the water."

The *Bon Accord*, she eased into a rhythm at exactly this point as she does on all good trips. The first twenty minutes she sounds rough—she's sizing up her fare for the day. She reflects her payload, offering noises and bangs on days when amusement is on tap and appreciation remains at bay.

We reached Cattle Point on the south end of San Juan Island one hour into the tour. The orcas were just around the corner, milling off South Beach. A four-mile stretch of coastline on the southern tip of San Juan Island, complete with every shape and manner of driftwood ever afloat. We eased to a gentle troll, four knots plus. L12, a sub-pod of the larger L pod, was feeding, spread out maybe four miles. We cut the engine, drifted, and enjoyed the moment. The orcas came no closer than one hundred fifty yards from the boat over the entire forty-five minutes we were there.

Only appreciation onboard—smiles and jubilant exclamations with each dorsal fin spotted. There were no breaches, no spyhopping, no lob-tailing, and most important, no tail-slapping. Those onboard appreciated what they witnessed: the orcas in their natural environment.

Did they leave disappointed because they failed to get "the shot" of a breach? No, they felt the power of the orcas, heard their breath, saw them in all their beauty. What is it that separates those that appreciate life and those that must conquer it or at the very least get a snapshot of it?

In reflecting on these trips, I looked for common ground and differences. What separates those that seek to learn and appreciate from those that seek purely amusement? We discussed the perils the orcas face, the challenges that lie ahead for their finned friends of the day. Through education, did the *Bon Accord* bring about appreciation for the orcas? Did I pass *Bon Accord* 101?

And what of the orcas? Will they endure an ever increasing population, a never ending pursuit by man to see all? Have we taken that "giddy" feeling, the one we experience at the ballpark, at a rock concert, at a birthday party for our kids, at the sight of a newborn, and exploited nature in pursuit of more?

We seem to have an endless thirst for amusement—more and more sporting events, more and more cable channels, more and more Little League games—yet what of education? Why do we not thirst for more as species? Why do we not seek to learn of our future, our evolution?

Threats

The life cycle of the salmon is an extraordinary tale and from time to time one comes across a book or passage that truly epitomizes this struggle. If I were to pinpoint my favorite read on the subject, it would surely be James A. Michener's story, Nerka the Salmon, found in both Alaska and Creatures in the Kingdom. The latter being a collection of Michener stories on animals as found in his novels.

In Nerka the Salmon, Michener describes the life cycle of an Alaskan sockeye salmon, from embryo to fry to fingerling to full fledged sockeye. He details their life's journey from the lake in which they are born, down the rivers to the Pacific and into the salt water.

The magnificent odds they face, the perils that exists at each phase of their lives, and most important, their fate. It's an adventure, a mystery, a horror, and a love story all in one.

I carry Creatures of the Kingdom on the *Bon Accord*. Stories about nature are ideal reading when you're curled up in a V-berth with the little ones, especially those with animals.

It's also a great referral for guests looking to learn more about the salmon and orcas.

The resident orcas of the San Juan Islands feed largely on salmon; it's believed to be 90 percent of their food source. They are every bit, if not more, important to the region as are the orcas. Their numbers by and large serve as a barometer to the health of these waters.

Salmon are born in natal spawning grounds, which may range many miles upriver and thousands of feet above sea level. Their life cycle begins as eggs that are fertilized in gravel nests (redds) in the summer months. Once the eggs hatch, young salmon use the lake or stream they are born in as a nursery of sorts, living here up to three years before heading downriver to the oceans.

The young salmon, or smolts as they are referred to at this stage, face incredible odds—predators, industry, hydroelectric dams, and mother nature all take a toll on their numbers. Of the four thousand eggs in a redd or nest, only a small fraction survive the first six months and an even smaller number remain after their frightful descent down the river some three years from birth.

Once the young salmon reach the sea, they enter the currents that stretch from Alaska to northern California, it's here they feed and grow to full-size adult salmon. It's here that seals, sea lions, and whales feed on them, further reducing their numbers.

After two years, the adult salmon begin their journey home. Back to the same natal spawning grounds from whence they came, up river, through rapids, over waterfalls. They cease to eat, driven by a purpose - to spawn a new generation of salmon. Once the females have laid their eggs and the male dutifully fertilizes them, they both die, no longer having the strength to swim. Most are eaten by predators—birds, bears and the like; many are left to decompose, offering nutrients back to the gravel that will spawn a new generation of young salmon.

It's these salmon the resident orcas of the San Juan Islands feed upon as they enter Puget Sound by way of the Strait of Juan de Fuca. To reach their spawning grounds, they pass by the west side of San Juan Island, making for large concentrations of salmon throughout the summer months. Take away the salmon, the food source of the orcas, and you take away the orcas.

Diminish the amount of salmon in Puget Sound, and other threats loom—toxins. The waters of Puget Sound were heavily laced with PCBs, DDT, dioxins, mercury, and other toxins at one time. While the factors that contributed to this buildup have been dealt with to some degree and many toxic waste sites are in a cleanup phase, large concentrations still remain along the food chain, buried in sediment under the water and landfills. These chemicals don't break down, but rather build up along the same food chain on which the orcas depend. Stored in fat, they're transferred from one living organism to the next, from worms to fish to orcas. These compounds impact the whales' immune systems and reproductive glands.

The relationship between salmon, toxins, and the orcas is especially important when salmon runs are low. The toxins are stored in the fat reserves of the orcas, the same reserves the orcas depend on when they go hungry from lack of salmon. As salmon runs decline, especially the chinook, the threat of toxins intensifies in the orcas.

A Sea Less Traveled

From the *Bon Accord*, little is learned below water of the salmon's fate. Our gaze is forever trained on the sea's surface. At times, we'll catch a glimpse of salmon jumping out of the water with orcas in hot pursuit, or one in the mouth of a seal or sea lion, their freshly torn flesh brightly coloring the landscape, reminding one of the rawness of nature and the inherent beauty to it all, the struggle of life and death.

We see other indications of salmon life: a bait ball of herring on the surface of the water, churned up into a frenzied pace by the salmon beneath and the seabirds above. A fleet of fisherman along the west side, pole curved, line taut, whoops and howlers onboard. A commercial netter heeled over twenty degrees, winch squeaking, shiny silver sparkles gathering in her holds, an occasional small one winged over the side.

Upon return to port, skinned and boned, salmon sit in a cooler at the fish market or for $19.95 on a menu at a local establishment. The question, one I try to answer onboard, is: do we assign value to the observation or do we merely enjoy them at face value?

Our ability to sustain life in the Puget Sound area depends on the salmon. So, do we look for a relationship to ourselves when we view them in the wild? It's the same question I ask in regard to the orcas, perhaps hoping their power and grace will make it easier to reflect upon.

We hear about dam removal, toxic waste site cleanup, and levels of PCBs in our food source. But, in this age of consumption, do we stop to ask why or how things came to be? How we've come to accept small percentages of toxins in our food as "relatively safe?" In our race to the finish, what propels us past common sense?

I've come up with one way to teach about the orcas and the salmon and the waters we sail on—a board game. The theme: San Juan Islands. The object: Move your boat, a thirty-foot scale replica of the *Bon Accord*, across the board, propelled by knowledge. The answers to the questions lie in the journey. Knowledge centers on questions about the region, about the environment.

The game parallels our voyage each day. The answers are there for those that pick up the card and accept the challenge in search of learning. It's a game; no one appears the fool for lack of knowledge.

Why do we place such a premium on this?

The goal or object of the game is to keep playing. There is no finish, no final wave, no final bell or whistle. The goal is to continue learning, accepting knowledge, searching for clues to stay in the game, understanding how life is sustained .

The Fleet

In the "fleet," every manner of tour boat plies the routes to and from the whales. Most operate May through October, since this is commonly known as the "season" for whale watching. A few of us operate year-round, selling our tours as "wildlife tours" in the winter months so as not to mislead passengers.

The *Bon Accord* is the prettiest boat in the fleet, no exception. I need no reminder as I sit, perched in her pilothouse, hand gripped on a varnished wood spoke wheel, surrounded by teak and mahogany trim, peering out onto a sea of machine-made craft.

Her sisters in trade come in all shapes and sizes, material and construction, design and theory—from rubber inflatable to what some would consider a small cruise ship. One even looks like a giant blue and yellow hot dog.

In Victoria. and Vancouver, British Columbia, passengers (up to twelve) travel in what we refer to as an inflatable or Zodiak, so named by brand. They are roughly thirty feet in length with an open cockpit. Passengers are stuffed into survival suits and strapped in, subjected to every jolt and bump these boats' twin and sometime triple outboard configurations can dole out over the waves. I suppose if there were an "E- ticket" ride out there, it would be these boats. Others auger in from the mainland with 300-plus onboard, bullhorns ablaze, directing passengers from side –to side, rolling under their weight as they race back and forth for a front row seat to view the orcas.

As most speed by or quickly toward and away from the *Bon Accord*, I often picture them all attached to equally spaced spokes, spinning around some geometric center—screaming passengers with their hands waving in the air, and orcas leaping over their heads.

Do we grow up or do we mature at about twelve years of age and spend the rest of our lives trying to duplicate those experiences we had in our youth, living our childhood over and over again, not only through our children, but also by way of experiences that make us feel "giddy"? Those experiences that amuse us, fill a void for us? In viewing a breach of the orcas, do we fill this void?

I played with boats in my youth, often pushing or pulling them in the water. I broke quite a few, too, and relished the task of putting them back together, making them sail again. There is no question the *Bon Accord* makes me "giddy" when I feel her glide through the water or after I've applied a new coat of oil to her rails.

Perhaps the whales in all their power and grace make us feel this way? Lost in our excitement, though, do we overlook a higher goal, one achieved through learning? Do we only associate education with work, not to interfere with our "play" or search for that "giddy" feeling? Has my search for this feeling led me to make it my life's work, to educate those seeking only amusement?

Through education, whale watch operators hope to form bonds between whale watchers and whales, and create a desire to help the orcas. Though, who defines education?

Most of the boats hire "naturalists" whose responsibility it is to educate. But the extent to which they educate people is not measured and largely remains unknown. To what extent do we accept that "giddy" feeling and direct its energy into a learning experience?

Naturalists point out the facts, life span, behavior, feeding, and which one is named "Ruffles." Yet, do they impart to those onboard an appreciation for the living medium they're encroaching upon for the day?

Do we educate if we take the time to inform passengers about conservation and about the perils the orcas face? In turn, if we gloss over these issues in favor and in search of that "giddy" feeling, do we fail as educators, merely providing amusement for none the betterment of the orcas? Are our pursuits genuine in this regard?

Of the thirty or forty boats that consistently tour the islands in search of the orcas, most belong to the Whale Watch Operators Association Northwest (WWOANW). The WWOANW publishes what is commonly referred to as the "guidelines." The guidelines provide instructions on how to operate a boat around the orcas. They are clear, although voluntary, with no real policing mechanism, at least not to date.

Each year, two organizations monitor boats around the orcas—Soundwatch and their Canadian counterpart, M3

(Marine Mammal Monitoring). Soundwatch is run through the Whale Museum in Friday Harbor. Both organizations are sorely underfunded and overmatched on the water.

The guidelines are straightforward, yet interpretation is far-fetched on the water. For the most part, a good percentage of the specific guidelines are followed. There is no question that without these guidelines there would be chaos around the whales. But are we better off instead of stricter, more enforceable guidelines?

There are many boats out there pursuing the whales, chasing that "giddy" feeling on a busy weekend, a three-day holiday. Competition for prime viewing space is limited, windows of opportunity small. As an operator you feel pressure, because it's an amusement ride, right? Orcas swimming under the boat are a large tip, right?

We all communicate with one another, at least those we have a relationship with. The *Bon Accord*, she listens in. She hears direction and locations of the orcas daily from her squawking VHF radio. She hears the whereabouts broadcast to anyone who has an ear for the information.

Unfortunately, boats unaware of the guidelines or how to operate around the pods thirst for a look at the whales, too. An ever growing fleet of private boaters is creating more and more confusion on the water. The tendency for these boats is to park in front of the whales' path, watch in amazement as they swim by and under, and then race around the pod and other boats to park in front of the whales a second time.

The guidelines state that vessels should avoid approaching closer than one hundred yards to any whale. This translates for a few boats into, "If I park the boat one hundred and one yards in front of the whales and turn the engine off, then I am not 'approaching' the whales."

This practice is becoming the norm on the water. Boats refer to it as "set up." "I'm going to set up (or park in front of the whales) here." It's a game of leapfrog with the orcas.

What of the orcas? Does anyone stop to ask what might the orcas think? I recently, while walking down a crowded street, raced in front of my wife and parked in front of her, "setup": I did this five times for amusement and eventually a sucker punch to the ribs. Do unto others as you'd have them do to you, right?

Orcas are highly intelligent. Isn't that partly their draw, the reason many seek a glimpse? It's not uncommon to see a line of boats "set up" for a mile, like an airport landing pattern. What does a sucker punch from a whale feel like?

For boats looking to parallel the orcas' swim from one hundred yards or more as prescribed by the WWOANW guidelines, which used to be the norm on the water, this not only puts pressure on those boat operators from their passengers—"Hey, look how close those boats are. Aren't you going to get that close?"—but it also negates the very thing we as whale watch operators claim to be providing, a look at the orcas in their natural environment. It is no more natural to see orcas swim through miles of rubber and plastic boats than to witness a breach as a spectator in a marine park.

Is parading the orcas through a string of rubber, plastic, wood, and aluminum boats akin to their "natural environment"?

And what of those boats that witness this behavior, those not privy to the "guidelines"? They arrive on the whales, witness this "set up" behavior, and think it is the normal way to operate around the whales.

Only, these private boaters in all their plastic fantastic glory don't turn their engines off. They park right on the whales, often from less than one hundred yards' approach, their engines spewing diesel exhaust into the orcas' path, hand on the throttle, ready to goose it if the whales get aggressive.

On a typical busy weekend day in the summer months, it is not uncommon to see fifty or more boats with the orcas. A few whale watching operators, a handful of commercial fisherman, a handful of recreational fisherman, a tug or two, a few cruisers, a few racing sailboats, and so on. At times, depending which path the orcas choose to travel, it can be chaotic on the water. It's odd—more boats, less space. Is it competition that drives us to be too close, within an arm's length, a stone's throw? From the *Bon Accord* we see more of the boats than they of us. We're small by comparison and our speed offers ample time to view boats as we approach. The *Bon Accord* doesn't race into a "set up" or flee the scene with any great speed. So from the wheel, we witness the haphazard nature boats operate around the whales. In some ways it mirrors the sensation I feel on the mainland highways—there is a rush on busy days. A competitive instinct fuels a desire to be too close. Coupled with an eagerness to please those onboard and the adrenaline the orcas stimulate, it's crazy on the water, boats literally racing each other to "set up" in front of the whales.

The question is, with three pods of orcas and fifty-plus boats, what are we selling? Are we selling a "natural environment" here? Perhaps some should go with the angle, "one-on-one relationship with the whales!" After all, there are eighty-three to go around and fifty-plus boats out there!

Yet, lost is the irony of the individuals involved. The captains, or at least those that have been around for years, who operate the WWOANW boats, are among the biggest sympathizers to the whales.

These captains are quick to point out private boaters breaking guidelines, report to Soundwatch or M3, quick to show remorse for anything that harms the whales, quick to show jubilation in new births, espouse the health of the pods when numbers are up, defend the orcas in all causes.

Have the whales brought them to this, or is this hints of passion from a relationship built up over the years? What is it that quells this passion for the pursuit of that "giddy" feeling for their passengers? Is it a large tip or the threat of lost wages for nonperformance?

Perhaps Maslov had it right when he cornered our needs for food, shelter, and health within a triangle. We strive to meet our basic needs, never truly looking to meet the needs of others or other living things. We take care of our needs, caring or at the very least appearing to care for the orcas only to protect our insecurities, not the well-being of another living creature?

Would an hourglass better reflect our pursuits in life? The upper chamber of which holds the sands of time and us racing, climbing to stay within our chamber, meet our basic needs. At the same time, we gloss over the needs of other living creatures, lest we be buried in the lower chamber by compassion, our efforts to protect the orcas.

There are a number of people who will argue that the boats in and around the whales do not affect their health.

And maybe they don't; perhaps it's in my learning to come? On the surface, their behavior doesn't appear to be defensive, other than a tail-slap here and there. Yet why does the "transient" whale shy away from boat traffic? I've heard it said of mammals that we habituate to our environment. Are those that follow this reasoning saying the "residents" have habituated to boat traffic, in turn boats don't hurt the whales?

Are we bringing the plastic tank to the whales, luring them closer to the boats with each passing season by our eagerness to be up close, within reach? Over the last twenty years of whale watching, have there been any studies done on the proximity of the whales to the boats? Is there a trend toward more whales more often being closer to the boats? At what rate are they habituating? I've heard captains relay that more and more super-pods are being sighted over the summer. These super-pods—gatherings of all three pods (J, K, L) together—are typically where males will congregate with females in the other pods, furthering the species, so to speak. To me this is a private act. Is there a chance the orcas are becoming too accustomed to our presence, habituated to the boats to the point where it's no longer a private act in their minds? All well and good for viewing, but where does this trend go from here? Are we leading the whales to us, enticing them to perform for our pursuits through our cheers and clicks? In the end, is this noble? How long will it be before a boat hits a whale?

Conservation

And what of the plight of the Orcas? I fear my tenure, with the Orcas, warrants careful attention. I am not an "advocate" for the Orcas and mostly have nothing in common with those that are, other than an appreciation for the Orcas existence and increased passion to protect them and if in doing I become an "advocate" so be it. I can only hope the *Bon Accord* steers me in the right direction.

There are a number of groups in and around the San Juan Islands working to protect marine mammals. I see hints of their presence from the wheel, read of their progress and see them out on the water. I admire their cause.

The Center for Whale Research, The Whale Museum, and The Orca Network to name a few, play a large role in the southern resident Orcas' future. Each is unique in their role, tied together by a common thread, the fate of the Orcas.

The Whale Museum's theme is natural history. Through education and research the goal of the Whale Museum is to encourage conservation, and stewardship of Washington's inland marine waters. Through art, from children's books to Native American teachings, the Whale Museum depicts northwest history along with science and the benefits of both toward fostering an understanding of the ecosystems we live in. Full size skeletal replicas, a theatre room, a reading room, and collection of artifacts and specimens relating to the whales are found upstairs in an interactive exhibit. Another program island kids enjoy, is Pod Nods. On three different nights, every other Saturday, young kids sleep over at the museum. Each night, the kids zero in on one of the three resident pods and learn about their characteristics.

From the wheel of the *Bon Accord*, I see the Whale Museum each day, atop the highest hill in town, overlooking the harbor. It's the last five minutes of the tour and, with each, I ask my passengers to visit the museum, if not that day, one of the days they have left on the island. It's rich in natural history, offers unique interactive exhibits and is to Friday Harbor what the Orcas are to the Puget Sound, without peer.

The Whale Museum also operates Soundwatch, and the on-the-water boater education program. The staff that operates Soundwatch works harder than anyone in the summer months. From a small inflatable with the word S O U N D W A T C H etched along its pontoons, they patrol the waters around the whales, quick to intercept boats or impede their progress when they become a threat to the whales. It's effective, but overmatched on the busy days. The Canadian M3 patrols on Soundwatch's days off. M3 also operates an inflatable pontoon type boat, yellow top on black pontoons.

One of the founding members of the Whale Museum, Kenneth Balcomb, created another project in 1976, Orca Survey, and is now Executive Director and Research Biologist for the Center of Whale Research. Orca Survey is a photo-identification survey of the Orcas in the San Juan Islands. Using both visual and acoustic recordings, researchers catalogue the whales. The data yields valuable information such as birth and mortality rates, keys to population studies and the overall health and welfare of the Orcas.

Orca Network, monitors the location of the Orcas in the Salish Sea and beyond by recording data phoned or emailed in as to the whereabouts of the whales at a given time. The Orca Network in turn, broadcasts these sightings over the email system to anyone with an eye for it. The Orca Network also sponsors and supports a number of events around the sound relating to the Orcas; symposiums, lecture series, fund raising, etc.

Outside of these organizations, there are a handful of other regional groups with an interest in the Orcas, some more vocal, some more vigilant in their approach, all equally impassioned with the fate of the Orcas.

On the government side, both NOAA (National Oceanic Atmospheric Association) and the National Marine Fisheries Service play a role in shaping the policies and laws that protect the marine mammals in Puget Sound. Never has that been more apparent than the last two years.

In June of 2002, National Marine Fisheries Service declared the southern residents to be "depleted" vs. "endangered." The latter would have afforded the whales more protection under the law.

In December of 2003, a judge in California, in a major victory for environmentalists, overturned this ruling. At issue in the 2002 decision, should the southern residents disappear, transients that surface in the islands at times would take their place. The judge in the 2003 ruling threw this argument out, finding that the southern residents are discrete from other populations - one of the benchmarks for protecting a species under the Endangered Species Act. This act also empowers environmental groups to bring lawsuits to force the government to protect a species under the act.

Superceding these listings and a law currently in place is the Marine Mammal Protection Act, which focuses on protecting mammals from direct harm or death. This act also contains provisions for a recovery plan, similar to the Endangered Species Act.

Where does the *Bon Accord* fit in? The key question and one I'm still trying to answer. I know there is a role for her in the Orcas plight. She knows the waters they swim contain some of the highest levels of toxins in the world. She feels the ebbs and flows of the salmon runs. She sees the ever-increasing boat traffic day-by-day. She's not in a position to lecture, to lobby, and certainly not fund a cause. To what degree am I?

She is in a position to educate those that seek her out.

Through education, there is hope, I think back to those days when I see the twelve-year old girl admire the Orcas from the bow of the *Bon Accord*, her delight in seeing them for the first time, her frustration when boats travel their path. Their captains from a previous generation, one hell bent in search of "giddy" not understanding.

Is this the age to zero in on for education? Somewhere between six and twelve lies the magic number for learning. At six, I witnessed my oldest change her focus on the boat. As with my two youngest, her focus was inside the cabin at age five. At age six, her focus is on the wildlife, the other boats, the waves, the wind, and the clouds. Questions roll off her tongue, the same questions I look to the *Bon Accord* for answers.

Between six and twelve, build a bond with the ecosystems, an appreciation for environments. Before this "next" generation, these twelve year olds can afford the pursuit of amusement in earnest.

At 13, too late, high school and expectations enter the picture, dilute the cause, and awake that part of the brain that seeks amusement. That part of the brain that hides conscience, wards off reflection, keeps guilt at bay. If in our youth, young children, we only find those who seek to understand our environment and those living creatures we share it with, and overall adult man is less passionate about this learning, than perhaps our education is wrought with misdirection. There is no connection between human emotions and evolution in learning. Does an eighth grader know the envelope of emotions or the concept of greed as it relates to life's chase? More important the trail of denial that follows in it's wake?

There is a demand for knowledge. We see it on the *Bon Accord* in young girls and boys. Yet, to say hope lies in the future, but not offer learning of human emotions as it affects the environment, is moving forward blinded by our pursuits, our search for amusement? To entrust children to understand this thought without teaching it passes only the buck, not knowledge.

To what end do we teach on the water? We offer characteristics of the Orcas, lifestyles, cultures, and behavior patterns. We don't explore what drives one to be on top of the Orcas, or what motivates one to be at an arm's length. It's part greed. It's part passion. It's part learning of our own emotions. A place most of us don't want to go.

If, perchance, our youth on the other hand welcomes learning of their emotions, emotions they later come to struggle with, then should we not empower them with an understanding or at the very least attempt to empower them to understand greed, passion, and their pursuits in life at an early age?

Perhaps, a class in conservation should be a prerequisite to entering high school. A careful look at all of life's food chains and how consumption affects them all. Not just consumption of food and drink, consumption of emotions, of feelings, consumption of that "giddy" feeling that leads us to prey on the environment.

Better yet, let's seek the wisdom of a twelve year old in coming up with a conservation plan. A twelve year old with no constituents, a twelve year old who as of yet is not living within his or her triangle, not looking to satisfy his or her basic needs.

Perhaps the answer rests in the air, in the water, or in the land we trod upon. The same source we seek dominion over, beckon to call our own. What in our makeup creates our thirst toward ownership? Do we seek dominion over the Orcas for in some way or another it presents a form of ownership? As with the land and the sea, why do we gloss over their needs in our chase in life?

To a 12 year-old a harbor seal popping up in a pristine cove holds meaning in their eye. Not a dollar value, an appraisal of worth in adult man's eye, but a meaning more pure and simple. It may be of a spiritual nature or something as simple as a smile. We see it on the *Bon Accord*, it need not be prompted or goaded, it 's far more simple, comes from within. There is a connection between the child and the seal and the water. The answer to our pursuits rests in this moment, this instant. If we can teach a 12 year-old to assess meaning rather than value to this moment, than perhaps education, in turn conservation stands a chance.

It's more than knowledge. It's an understanding that all threads in life are connected at any given point in time. The waters, land and air are dependent, living creatures with basic needs. To heap content on one, affects another. To rape one of its fruit, labors another.

Maybe this wisdom would not be lost on a twelve year old. A girl or boy who has yet to learn how to assess value, yet to learn what money can buy, to associate money and amusement in pursuit of that "giddy" feeling.

If we fail to educate at this level, if we seek to impart this wisdom at a later stage, the message becomes diluted, fades into the background, scribbled on a notebook. At thirteen and beyond, we live within our triangle; our basic needs are first and foremost on our mind, our bias is too strong.

Perhaps I am naïve, and again my brief tenure warrants careful consideration. It's not science or conservation in it's current form that will save the Orcas, free them from those in search of that "giddy" feel, free them from those that sell amusement, pay no fare.

The Orcas don't need to be saved. It's us that need to be saved from our pursuits. Will the Orcas show the way? The *Bon Accord* hears their wisdom? Wisdom obtained over millions of years, from land mammal to ocean king. Perhaps this will be man's fate, evolve into cetacea humanis, and in doing we must clear the seas of all top predators en route.

A Sea Less Traveled

A sea change is needed for the Orcas, for life in the sound. The answer to their survival lies in our living, not in their dying. Our dumping of chemicals, our use of pesticides, our thirst for energy, our desire to own waterfront property, our desire to own bigger and faster boats, our desire to build dams to harness nature's energy. Each of these is a byproduct of our chase in life, driving our pursuits. Our insecurity fuels this chase, confuses them with our basic needs in life.

Conclusion

It's late winter, early spring approaches; the *Bon Accord* is set to sail tomorrow with a group of two and a family of four. The wind is howling outside, at least thirty knots. Forecast for tomorrow: only ten knots out of the south, slight chance of rain. A typical January day in the islands.

The *Bon Accord* is weathering the winter months just fine. Her blisters in her cabin side have opened. Yet, they remain small and will be easily handled in the warmth of spring. Her mast came down during one particular frontal system that moved through, bent the gooseneck on her boom. Some knucklehead, namely me, left her awning up. No worries; I'll have her up in time for the nor'easter that will hit this month to test her strength and my resolve. She seems to be riding a little high in the water, her boot stripe or waterline stripe offering a little more of itself than usual. No doubt the absence of people on board, empty water tanks, and minimal fuel in her holds the reason. She's been quiet the past few months, patiently at rest in her slip. I visit her a few times each week, make up reasons to seek shelter down at the docks. There is more quiet time in the harbor, more time to reflect on things. The whales haven't been around lately, or at least off the *Bon Accord*. I heard L pod passed by Lime Kiln the other night, or was it J pod? In any event, we'll cast off tomorrow in search of Orcinus orca in what will be the first tour of the new year. There was a lot of talk about the whales this off-season, with many a soapbox champion crawling out of the woodwork.

In looking back over the past two seasons, and looking for thoughts on the summer ahead, I'm not sure I'm any closer to figuring out this puzzle than I was six months ago. I've come to a few conclusions—some warrant more thought, others nary a consideration. I also fear my want of understanding may subside as the season picks up and more and more come to see the whales. How will I react this summer?

The southern resident pods seem to be stable in numbers according to those in the know, with three consecutive years of population gain. Healthy salmon runs seem to be by and large the consensus on why they've fared well as of late—an increase of chinook in these waters, spurned along by hatcheries. I'm not sure I understand how anyone can calculate the health and welfare of a living creature that has been around since prehistoric times. To say they are stable in numbers after sampling only a little over thirty years of data seems a bit naive. In any event, they're more qualified than I to make that assumption.

In writing this book, I was awed by the power and grace of the orcas, and stumped by the behavior of some who seek to prey on them for amusement. It inspired me to tell of this tale. If in this voice I seem a little more passionate than in the body of this work, it's only after reading in whole that I realized I may have been too soft on us, myself included, as a race or species.

I do believe our pursuits are driving us to the end of the earth, to places with dragons, and I believe we seek only amusement in most of these pursuits. It's not to say science and knowledge are not important—they are. It's the value we assign to some of this knowledge, in leaving it to other generations to calculate, that scares this captain. You hear it said over and over, "Hope lies in the next generation; the future looks bright." What are we teaching this next generation that we ourselves weren't taught?

Living in the San Juans has changed my life, offered a new perspective. The *Bon Accord* has brought me to new heights in terms of understanding my life's chase. Combined, the islands and a small wooden boat offer a unique existence, one long absent in years prior, hints of which I felt in my youth. To say it's a spiritual one, I can't say with a lot of conviction. I'm not sure what a spiritual existence is. If my ying and yang are in balance, so be it. It's part fear in discovery and exploration. It's part sensory in mind and spirit, visual and acoustic images. It's part freedom, the opportunity to discover and explore. Or maybe, just maybe, the devil's at play in an idle mind? I'm sure more than one who reads this will claim my leisure affords too much imagination.

In looking for ways to explore learning, ideas for education on the *Bon Accord*, ways to bring about change in our learning, the answers seem apparent, the means less so. How does one start from scratch to develop learning in a system so dependent on fact and fiction and very little in between? I've tried to use the other boats, islands, wildlife and all else we see out on the water to gauge reaction and response. I've quizzed kids on the orcas and their behavior—what did they see and how did it make them feel? For the most part, I've collected data: bits and pieces of human behavior, actions and reactions, concepts and ideals. I'm not sure how much I've stored—at the very least, it was enough to impassion me to write this book. I can't help but feel the gap, though, the one that bridges the answers and the questions. It's a nagging feeling, helpless at times. It's in the daydreams, the aimless thought on a beautiful day. I see it in the *Bon Accord*, in the teak work, in the paint blisters, in her lines. In the islands, the secluded bays and coves, the evergreen forests, the blue waters. In the wildlife, the delicate balancing of the seal, the winged flight of a cormorant, the breach of the orcas.

Is it power, the raw exhibition of force in the orcas' breach? Are we awed by this? At the point of witnessing this power, what triggers that "giddy" feeling? Is it the thought of holding dominion (greed) over this power, the thought (self-indulgence) of this power being on display for us? Or is it the thought of being able to relay the witnessing (empowering) of this power to another, through photo or tall tale? Where do these feelings fall in our triangle? Does being empowered, the thought of self-indulgence, or chasing greed fall under our basic needs? Why have we so departed from our basic pursuits—food and shelter? It's as if these emotions have taken hold of us, altered our pursuits in life, and left us chasing more. A fiery dragon within, the one warned of in the charts.

Conclusion

Do we face the dragon in teaching life's chase to children? It's a powerful symbol, much like the orcas, a magnificent beast without peer, one slain in myth only. Or do we hide from the dragon within? Seek solace in our pursuits, life's chase?

The tone herein will ruffle a few feathers in the islands, on both sides of the fence, no doubt. There is no message or conclusion in this work, though, only thought and inquiry. I'm not one who wishes to see whale watching stopped. I believe it has value. There are those who claim it harms the whales and there are those who claim nothing bothers the whales. To me the answer probably lies somewhere in the San Juan Islands and everyone in life should have the opportunity to experience life's treasures, including watching the orcas.

It's a magical place, without peer, really. For those looking for the pot of gold under the rainbow, it may very well exist in these islands. There are enough rainbows offering hope. I believe each of us sees in a rainbow what we hope to find in life—a pot of gold, a spiritual existence, a romantic vision, or some other imagery hoping to be quantified. If in children's books and fables we take that pot of gold and turn it into a content soul, would our pursuits be driven by material greed, a thirst for more and more amusement? It's the same puzzle, different characters.

Will I sell a chance to see the orcas this year? On paper, or in rack cards perhaps, but I'm hoping the *Bon Accord* will lead me down another path, a sea less traveled. I'm hoping to bridge that gap between the answers in my head and the questions the *Bon Accord* has placed in my path.

~ *Smooth Sailing!*

References

David Richardson
Magic Islands
Orcas Publishing Co.
Eastsound, WA 98254

Evelyn Adams
San Juan Islands Wildlife
The Mountaineers
Seattle, WA

The American Cetacean Society
Field Guide to the Orca
Sasquatch Books
Seattle, WA

Richard Osborne, John Calambokidis,
Eleanor M. Dorsey

A Sea Less Traveled

A Guide to Marine Mammals of Greater Puget Sound
The Whale Museum
Friday Harbor, WA

Chuck Flaherty
Whales of the Northwest
Cherry Lane Press
Seattle, WA

James A. Michener
Creatures of the Kingdom
Random House
New York

Seabirds of the World
Peter Harrison
Christopher Helm Publishers Ltd.,
Imperial House 21-25 North St.
Bromley, Kent BR1 1SD

The Whale Museum
62 First Street North
Friday Harbor, WA 98250
www.whalemuseum.com

Orca Network
2403 S. North Bluff Rd.
Greenbank, WA 98253
www.orcanetwork.org

The Center for Whale Research

References

PO Box 1577
Friday Habor, WA 98250
www.whaleresearch.com

Bon Accord Tours
PO Box 994
Friday Harbor, WA 98250
www.bonaccord.com

Acknowledgements

This book could not of been published without the help of American Book Publishing staff, namely Tenille Martin (editor) for her patience and understanding, Margie Schlatter (copy edit) for her wit, Jana Rade (cover design) for her ability to capture the emotion herein by design, C.L. Nunn for her love of wood boats (operations) as well as Jan Judd (marketing) and all others with American Book Publishing that lent their expertise and knowledge to this project. I'd also like to thank Kari Koski and Dr. Rich Osborne with the Whale Museum and Susan Berta for their time, consideration and advice. Most of all, I'd like to thank the people of the San Juan Islands, all those that offered a smile over the past two years, for without them there would be no inspiration. Finally, many thanks to my father for putting a few wings on this nut! And special thanks, as well as humble appreciation, for the southern resident orcas.

About the Author

Patrick Pillsbury, U.S.C.G. licensed master, is captain of the *Bon Accord* in Friday Harbor, Washington. At thirty-eight, he has worked on and sailed the Pacific for most of his life, including two transpacific crossings and over 10,000 miles of open ocean sailing. His passion in life is all things family and boats and the waters they float. He lives in Friday Harbor on San Juan Island in Washington with his wife and three daughters.